P9-DIG-923

The Second Bud

The story of Tiger Mountain Vineyards is a window into the nascent community of regional and local wineries; Martha and John are helping to craft a high-quality wine industry in America's rural South.

—Doug Frost, master sommelier,
master of wine, author,
and internationally known wine consultant

Second Bud is vintage Martha Ezzard: detailed and passionate prose with a splash of humor. She recounts her family's pioneering venture into the world of fine wine from the terroir of a Southern family farm.

—Lea Donosky,
former Sunday editor,
Atlanta Journal-Constitution

Martha Ezzard never shied away from difficult subjects as a newspaper columnist, but who'd have expected to find her making award-winning wines from grapes grown on a North Georgia family farm—digging in the dirt in Tiger, Georgia. Her fascinating story is not just about a change in lifestyle but a leap of faith.

—Dick Denny, past chairman,
High Museum of Art, founder and chief taster,
High Museum Atlanta, wine auction

At Tiger Mountain Vineyards Martha Ezzard has proven herself to be a talented and tireless promoter, event planner, tour guide, tasting expert, and grape harvester. While I have appreciated her efforts in all these capacities, I do miss the thoughtful editorials she used to write for the *Atlanta Journal-Constitution*. What a pleasure to page through this memoir of her life as a winemaker and read her elegant, incisive, and ever-opinionated prose again.

—John Kessler, award winning food writer
and chief restaurant critic, *Atlanta Journal- Constitution*

Endowed by
TOM WATSON BROWN
and
THE WATSON-BROWN FOUNDATION, INC.

The Second Bud

Deserting the City for a Farm Winery

Martha M. Ezzard

MERCER UNIVERSITY PRESS
MACON, GEORGIA

MUP/H875

1400 Coleman Avenue
Macon, Georgia 31207

First Edition

Books published by Mercer University Press are printed on acid-free paper that meets the requirements of the American National Standard for Information Sciences—Permanence of Paper for Printed Library Materials.
Mercer University Press is a member of Green Press Initiative (greenpressinitiative.org), a nonprofit organization working to help publishers and printers increase their use of recycled paper and decrease their use of fiber derived from endangered forests. This book is printed on recycled paper.

Library of Congress Cataloging-in-Publication Data

Ezzard, Martha M., 1938-
The second bud : deserting the city for a farm winery / Martha M. Ezzard. -- First edition.
pages cm
Includes index.
ISBN 978-0-88146-455-9 (paperback : acid-free paper) -- ISBN 0-88146-455-4 (paperback : acid-free paper)
1. Ezzard, Martha M., 1938- 2. Vintners--Georgia--Tiger--Biography. 3. Women vintners--Georgia--Tiger--Biography. 4. Vineyards--Georgia--Tiger. 5. Wineries--Georgia--Tiger. 6. Farm life--Georgia--Tiger. 7. Family farms--Georgia--Tiger. 8. Tiger (Ga.)--Biography. 9. Tiger (Ga.)--Social life and customs. 10. Career changes--United States--Case studies. I. Title.
TP547.E88A3 2013
663'.20092--dc23
[B]

2013027491

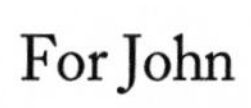

For John

Contents

Acknowledgments

Too many people are part of the fabric of this book to acknowledge them all. Without generations past in our family and community who cultivated and cared for the Arrendale-Ezzard land at Tiger, there would be no Tiger Mountain Vineyards.

I am grateful to those who have contributed their professional talents over the past four years to helping me shape this story in a form I can now share:

My first editor, Allison McCabe, who taught me that writing a book is not like writing a newspaper column;

Marc Jolley, director of Mercer University Press, whose enormous enthusiasm for my story was key to its completion; also, Marsha Luttrell, publishing assistant, and Mary Beth Kosowski, marketing director;

Photographer Peter McIntosh, whose love of the North Georgia mountains and our vineyards is reflected in the timeless moments of light and beauty he captures;

Ginny Heckel, whose photographs of people and events are always connected to her love of nature and of joyful gatherings.

Special gratitude to my husband John who was born with the heart of a farmer and who pours his love of land into the dirt and vines and grapes at Tiger Mountain.

To our three children, Shelly, Lisa, and John Jr., for their commitment to our vineyard venture, the farm at Tiger, and for their encouragement in the writing of this book; and to our six grandchildren who are the seventh generation to fall in love with the farm at Tiger.

Thanks to our small staff, who have endured my "don't interrupt" moments: Jabe Hilson, Jon Engel, Judy Ruth, and Tristen Vanhoff.

Finally, I thank our winery partners and dear friends, John and Marilyn McMullan, for their encouragement while writing this book.

Preface

"Did you always dream of having a vineyard?" asks my young Atlanta friend, as she and her fiancé follow me up the winding gravel road to our house to find a basket for their freshly picked blueberries. We pause to examine a cluster of Malbec, already hanging purple, the August sun dancing on its leafy canes.

It's a question I hear over and over again, one I often wish I could just answer with a nod.

That would be misleading, though. John and I had no intention of starting a vineyard when we decided to transform our lives in order to save his family farm in the Blue Ridge Mountains of Georgia. I had laughed in disbelief when he first raised the idea. Grow *wine* grapes in the rural *Bible belt*? This was the land where our parents, on both sides, had been avowed teetotalers, sipping grape juice at communion as lifelong Baptists and Methodists do. I'd reminded him that my father suffered an annual scolding from my South Georgia mother for drinking a single glass of wine at the office Christmas party. She routinely poured hers in a flowerpot when no one was looking.

A red-tailed hawk flying over the vineyard saves me momentarily from having to answer my friend's question. We pause to admire the splendid bird. I look once more at the familiar silhouette of our wine grape trellises, standing like soldiers marching in line toward Tiger Mountain, a battalion of protectors watching over the young Cabernet Franc vines planted on hills where rows of sweet corn once stood. I've come to love that crooked mountain, a near sacred symbol for my husband, whose family has farmed in its shadow for five generations. I still have to pinch myself when I look at our lush green vines, the seventy-five-year-old barn wearing its new coat of red paint, and the roses blooming madly at the end of each row of grapes. I marvel that the vineyard John wanted is a reality. It hasn't been a smooth ride, though—far from it. Before moving to Tiger I'd never lived in a small town. I had always been an urban dweller, content with a Starbucks and a Sunday *New York Times*. I prefer my greens in a bowl at "Lettuce Surprise You," a salad bar near my Atlanta condominium rather than from manure-rich earth. Still, with our three children grown and out of college, John and I undertook a grand venture. Neither of us dared leave our day jobs while we planted vines with our own hands (our only help was Arvel Holmes, a retired football coach who worked for John's dad for twenty years, who often suggested that "Maahtha oughta go on back to the city"), but both of us resolved to cultivate something that will reflect our particular passion: we want to save a piece of earth, not just any piece of earth, but the hundred acres at Tiger Mountain that are part of John's soul.

Has a vineyard always been our dream? "No," I reply. "Not always…."

The Second Bud

1

Plant Wine Grapes in the Bible Belt?

> The vine shall give her fruit...and the heavens shall give their dew. —*Zechariah 8:12*

When you drive from Atlanta to Tiger, population 339, you turn left on the Tiger Connector from the new Highway 441 onto the narrow, winding Old Highway 441. At the four-way stop, you run squarely into the post office and the Tiger Food Mart. Less than two hours from the city, Tiger is a place of pastoral hills, lakes, and mystical blue ridges. It's a land of seasonal extravaganzas, from the pink and white splash of spring dogwood and mountain laurel to the bold show of fall hardwoods, native red maple, yellow hickory, and orange sourwood. Today, visitors to our vineyards can spot the turn-off to Tiger by keeping an eye out for Goats-on-the-Roof produce market on the corner of the main highway and the Tiger Connector. If there are children along, they'll want to stop and feed the goats—Bella, Della, Speckles, Elvis and Dolly—that graze on the grass roof of the rustic market. I remember when that corner was less colorful, when it was marked only by the faded blue sign of Ramey's filling station, a spot where locals worked on old cars and chewed the fat.

On a trip to Tiger to visit my father-in-law after I had made a risky decision to leave Denver, our family home for twenty-three years, to take a job with the *Atlanta Journal-*

Constitution, I head toward my husband's hometown on a brilliant October Saturday morning. The familiar spots are mostly unchanged from the time of my initial visit when John and I first started dating: the Tiger Food Mart is touting the best sausage biscuits in the world; The Old Store still displays Georgia Bulldog birdhouses and T-shirts on tables outside; Geneva's beauty parlor is as busy as ever in its gussied up trailer with a voluptuous garden in front. I pass the familiar white clapboard of the Church of God with the sign in front that says "JESUS SAVES" in faded red letters. Candler's gravel plant and the Tiger Volunteer Fire Station are much the same. The once-deserted cow pasture beside it is today the Tiger Drive-In, recently rebuilt to look just as it did thirty years ago. I saw *Thunder Road*, the moonshine movie starring Robert Mitchum, at this hot spot. Moonshine and coming to Jesus are *very* Tiger. So are conversations about garden manure over a cheeseburger and sweet tea at the Tiger Food Mart; so is the weekly news from the Tiger postmaster about who's seen black bears where; and so, as the future unfolds, are picnics under the old oak trees overlooking the Ezzard vineyards, featuring local cheeses and locally grown wines (namely, ours)—just up the road from the drive-in.

But on this trip to Tiger, shortly after I left my Denver law practice to take a newspaper job in Atlanta, planting a vineyard or starting a winery in this tiny conservative North Georgia community isn't something that has ever occurred to my husband or me. I am driving up from Atlanta this October Saturday simply to check on John's dad, Retired Lt. Colonel William Trimble Ezzard, whom we call "Poppa" and friends call "the Colonel." He's able to putter around the family farm, but his health is failing. His wife, Ruth, died the year before, and Poppa hasn't been the same since. Keeping the farm going is a growing family concern, and I intend to make frequent weekend visits since John is still in Colorado.

My notion of unending idyllic weekends at the farm, however, is already starting to bump up against the reality of finding a way to make the farm pay for itself. Everyone in John's family, his sisters and brother especially, know Poppa can't keep the land cultivated the way he used to. Without farm income for basic upkeep, and with land prices and property taxes going up…well, the pressure to sell could soon outweigh family sentimentality. After John's mom died, there were discussions about this. Dividing the land or selling some of it wasn't acceptable to anyone. A gated development or golf course replacing the red barn and hayfields, or houses with pseudo-stone fountains replacing the old farm pond, home to bass and blue gill, wild geese and heron, would be a family tragedy. But it seemed clear even then that only John was situated to keep the hundred-acre farm together were we to decide we could afford to buy out the siblings and other heirs. We were uneasy about taking on new debt in our fifties, and we were taking a financial hit anyway, with my career change from lawyer to journalist. "Eventually, somebody in this family has got to live in Tiger if we want the farm to survive development pressures," John had said to me on the phone the previous evening.

So I have conflicting emotions as I drive into my husband's tiny hometown again. Less than a year earlier I had written a letter to Ron Martin the editor of the *Atlanta Journal-Constitution*, whom I had never met, telling him I was weary of writing motions and briefs. I enclosed some writing samples, telling John I had put a note in a bottle and sent it off to the ocean. Eight months later, incredibly, I received an offer to become an opinion writer for the Atlanta newspaper where I once interned as a college journalism student. I might not have accepted a position in New York or San Francisco, but Atlanta is my hometown. Though I have no family there today, it's close to Tiger. John was already traveling to Tiger more now that his dad was alone and getting on in years. Together we decided we could survive a commuter marriage. I would move to Atlanta and give a new career a whirl while John stayed in Denver pondering what to do long-term about the family farm. We set no deadlines on each other and resolved not to let more than two weeks go by without a weekend together.

So far, our new lifestyle is working for us. I had never lived alone, so I had to get over the shock of not being as self-sufficient as I thought I was: I couldn't figure out how to put the bed together when my furniture arrived; I couldn't get the television cables hooked up right. But I relish scribbling column ideas on a yellow pad as I admire Atlanta's sparkling skyline from my mid-town balcony late at night. I'm happy to be liberated from the unending motions, briefs, and legal memos that can stifle creative thoughts. And since I've taken to checking in on Poppa, Tiger is a nice break from the city hubbub.

I took my very first trip there with John when he was a freshman in medical school and I was a student at the University of Georgia. When we drove through town, he pointed out Syrup City Road, a narrow lane that was once the wooded site for stills belonging to well-known moonshiners. ("*Syrup*—get it?" he said, guessing correctly that an Atlanta girl wouldn't grasp mountain moonshine lingo.) His grandparents were overseeing the farm while his father was stationed in Germany. I couldn't wait to see this quaint place John had talked about so much, and I really wanted to taste the Ezzard blueberries he often bragged about.

As we pulled up to the farm, the gravel crunched beneath our tires in a series of uneven bumps, and, for the first time, I saw the rock house up the hill, the house where John had grown up when his father was running the family dairy farm. The multi-hued rocks and gabled roof gave it an English cottage look that I hadn't expected to find in Georgia's Appalachian Mountains. John proudly told me his father and grandfather sledded the rock down from Tiger Mountain with a mule and built the house when he was a baby. On the porch, framed with arches on two sides, were four inviting rocking chairs with worn, quilted pillows of different patterns and a couple of flower baskets hanging on crooked wires. I could see Grandma Tallulah standing in the doorway. She was wearing a gingham apron, and she took both of my hands in hers as we met on the small porch. Her fluffy white hair was translucent in the sunlight, her light blue eyes the shade of stone-washed denim. John gave her a hug and introduced me. Then he asked immediately about the blueberries.

"I think they're the best they've ever been, son," she replied with a laugh. "Now you two make yourselves comfortable," she said. "I just made iced tea with fresh mint," she added and headed off to the kitchen. We followed on her heels.

As we passed through the cozy living and dining room area I noticed there were stacks of magazines and papers on every surface and a colorful crocheted afghan on the back of the worn living room sofa.

"If we pick blueberries will you make us a cobbler?" John asked, as he accepted his glass of tea.

She nodded, offered me tea, and invited me to sit down. Then she promised to find a jar of her newly made blackberry jam for me to take home. I felt as if I had known her for ages, not minutes.

"You heard about Ma Clyde's fall, didn't you, son?" she asked, getting out a deep-dish cobbler pan and canisters of flour and sugar. "She'd be mighty pleased if you'd stop by on your way out."

"How's Uncle Bumps and the pecans?" John asked, after he agreed to the visit. I giggled over the name, Bumps. They didn't hear me.

"It's been pourin' rain the whole month down in Quitman," she replied. "It's no good for his pecan crop. I reckon we could use some of that rain up here."

She and John covered the status of every living cousin while I sat at the dining room table leafing through the yellowed pages of a Methodist Women's Auxiliary cookbook. I had never known either of my grandmothers, and I felt a little envious at their comfortable rapport. John's grandfather, I learned, had gone over to neighboring Lakemont to do some surveying for another farmer.

Finally, John and I darted out the back door with some cut-off half-gallon milk cartons his grandmother gave us to pick blueberries by the pond. The cartons each had crocheted ties secured to the handles, ties long enough for us to wrap around our waists for hands-free picking. I remarked on how quaint and charming it was to spend time crocheting such things, so I was chastened when John replied that his grandmother had been a suffragette and a founder of the county's first League of Women Voters.

Just like they did on that day thirty-five years earlier, the red leaves on the blueberry bushes across the road from the farmhouse and the old creamery building glisten in the morning sun as my car rounds the curve past the Candler gravel plant. I turn left at the simple building with a tiered wooden vegetable stand in front, which once served as the creamery for the dairy business. It has "EZZARD" painted on it in black letters. To locals this farm building by the road is a familiar symbol of fresh vegetables for sale and berry picking on the honor system. The old wooden box Poppa made twenty years ago for the berry money is in its familiar place, lock ajar as it often is.

When I arrive at the house, Poppa gets up from his rocking chair on the front porch to greet me as I drive up. So does his dog, Tippy, his constant companion. Tippy, who is part Chow and part Husky, licks me ferociously and pants, displaying the black spot on the tip of her tongue for which John's mom named the once-stray puppy.

"I'm glad to see you, girl," Poppa says, taking my hand in his.

He looks somewhat rumpled—what worn farm shirt or pants he wears are never his concern—but now he looks thinner, and he leans on a cane to greet me. One side of his face is slightly distorted from the Bell's palsy he suffered almost two years ago.

I kiss his check. "And I'm glad to see you're still sharing your breakfast with Tippy," I reply, looking at the bits of grits and scrambled eggs in her dish on the front porch. (Tippy is the only dog I've ever known to like grits.)

Poppa sits down and reaches for the brush he keeps on the windowsill to brush Tippy. "Make yourself at home," he says with a grin.

I take my bag to the tiny upstairs bedroom, where I open the casement window and push the heavy drapes to one side. Once back downstairs, I brew a pot of coffee, offering Poppa a cup.

We sit on the porch together, sipping, while I share the particulars of my new job at the newspaper. Poppa is an avid reader of the *Atlanta Journal-Constitution*, and I can tell he is pleased that I've given up lawyering and am writing again. For lifelong farmers and most rural dwellers, in fact, lawyers are entirely too "slick."

"Have you met Furman Bisher?" he asks.

He is referring to the legendary sports columnist, an institution at the paper. I tell him my editor is Jim Wooten and that I've met Celestine Sibley, both of whose columns he reads, but have yet to meet Furman.

After he finishes brushing Tippy, Poppa takes a tattered notebook out of his pocket. Some of the pages are yellowed, but each has a neat column of dates, rainfall, and temperature written in his scrawled hand, some in pencil and some in ink. Pointing with his cane to the acreage across the road from the farmhouse, cultivated in hay and berries, he notes that the raspberries could stand thinning this fall. "They just grow to beat the band when we have as much rain as we've had this month," he says, shaking his head, jotting down a note and then slipping the book back into his pocket.

Poppa stands, leaning on his cane for a moment, and then walks slowly down the porch steps; Tippy follows contentedly. He tells me he needs to examine the yellowed leaves on three apple trees close to the house. They produced very few apples this year. I head back into the kitchen and notice the fridge is fairly empty, so I decide to make a quick trip to Andy's Market in nearby Clayton. I love Andy's; the small grocery carts and brown paper sacks of local water-ground cornmeal tied with string give it country character.

When I return, I pull out the well-used iron skillet in the kitchen cupboard and make Poppa a pone of corn bread. I cook some fresh green beans too, then open a jar of homemade applesauce I discover in the small pantry that is still filled with several years' worth of jams, jellies, zucchini relish, and watermelon rind preserves John's mom made before she passed away. I pick up a jar of raspberry jam and note the dated label in her handwriting. For a moment, I can hear the bustling sounds and smell the aromas that made Ruth's small kitchen so inviting. I set two places in the dining room for us to have lunch. When Poppa comes inside he thanks me for fixing his "dinner." The mid-day meal at the farm is always "dinner" even though "supper"—at least when John's mom was living—was no small salad.

Afterward, Poppa takes a nap and I go for a long walk, soaking in the familiar sights of the farm: the old gray barn, faded and much the worse for wear since Ruth passed away, and beside it the magnificent and unchanged cement silo. I marvel anew at the pond behind the farmhouse, its reliable reflection of Tiger Mountain, the 2800-foot-high wonder from which the town gets its name. Some say it was named after a Cherokee chief; others say the cries of mountain lions reminded early British and Scottish explorers of the cries of tigers. My husband contends the mountain viewed from afar looks like a crouched tiger. I hike a short, narrow loop on the mountain at leisurely pace. Folks rarely hurry in Tiger—John's late cousin Lester described Tiger as a place where things are "bout like common." I stop just above the Concord grape vineyard on the hill to pick fall wildflowers: purple ironweed, golden rod, wild blue asters, and a few late-blooming Joe-Pye weed. When I return to the farmhouse, I put the flowers in two stoneware pitchers, one on the dining room table and one in the little upstairs room where I always sleep. When Poppa wakes from his nap, he admires the deep color of the ironweed.

"It's been a better year for flowers than for sweet corn," he says. "Too much rain and too many worms. Can't get around to hoeing all the corn like we used to, either."

That night as I move some books from the table by my bed, I stumble on a yellowed newspaper article about Poppa that is tucked in one of the books. It's a column from 1972 by Bob Harrell of the *Atlanta Journal*, a legendary writer of Georgia places and people. Harrell roamed the state writing a weekly "Dateline Georgia." "In the Land of Berries" is the title of his column about Poppa, who is pictured holding two baskets of strawberries and commenting, "Frost knocked the blossoms off the blueberries." I am fascinated with how well Harrell captured Poppa's connection to the land in such a short piece, a connection that lives on in my husband, who would find it impossible to greet spring without getting his hands in the earth.

> Now Mr. Ezzard tills this land...and despite the fact that he was alone out there in the field, he had the company of that which he had worked with for many years, the earth, his plants. Of course, Mr. Ezzard does not talk with the earth and the plants in the sense that we talk with each other, but I believe there is a special communication.... When Mother Nature speaks, Mr. Ezzard listens, watches and always tries to soothe the land if her words are hard.... (May 24, A-8)

I fall asleep, wondering if I will ever feel that connection to the Tiger earth that runs in my husband's veins as it does Poppa's. I know for sure, especially when I go to a potluck meal with some of John's relatives where the women all swap recipes, that I have little in common with some aspects of country life.

The next day, I offer to take Poppa to church. He and Ruth had been active in the Clayton United Methodist Church ever since John was a baby. Everyone greets us warmly, and Poppa pulls out his pocket watch and commends the young preacher afterward for getting church out by noon. Back at the farm, I drive Poppa out to check on the old Yates apple tree past the barn, beyond rows of spent corn stalks on the hillside. The tree, once part of an orchard Poppa planted before he was called to duty in World War II, resembles a giant umbrella, its tiny red apples hanging in polka dot design, teasing the clouds above. Poppa picks a couple of low hanging apples for me, then leans against the tree trunk as if connecting with an old friend.

"They're better after the first fall frost," he says.

I bite into the sweet red apple whose speckled skin is no match for the shiny Red Delicious apples in grocery store bins. What commends the humble Yates apple is that the skin bleeds into the sweet, crisp pulp as you take a bite, as if to say "take all of me just as I am." A flock of geese fly overhead in perfect formation. It occurs to me that the musky smell of decaying leaves and fermenting apples already fallen to the ground, the rays of sunlight dancing through white pines on the mountain, and the honking geese are inseparable from the land itself. They make me think of my husband, who loves the smell of an Appalachian fall. If he were here, he'd scoop up a handful of musky leaves to feel and smell his familiar piece of earth.

"There are plenty of years when the apple trees get nipped in a spring cold spell," says Poppa, tapping his cane lovingly on the old apple tree's crooked trunk, "but come fall, the Yates are as sweet as any apple there is."

We return to the farmhouse and the telephone is ringing. It's Cousin Janie Pleasants Taylor (known as Janie P.), who lives down the road, calling to invite me to a "family feed" the following weekend. I politely decline—too many relatives I can't possibly navigate without John.

"Too bad you can't stay another night and come to the quilting club tomorrow," Janie P. suggests, knowing that quilting isn't my thing and never will be. Still, the invitation I know is her way of including me in the Tiger community.

As I hang up, I gaze out the living room window at the autumn colors on the mountain and wish I could stay; I'd like to take a longer hike in the woods, or walk around the pond at dawn to see the mist rising in silent swirls. In my head I begin to write a column for the newspaper using the old Yates apple tree—a tree my husband remembers playing in as a boy—as a metaphor for how some things about my native South never change.

"I'd hate to see you driving to the city after dark."

Poppa's words send me scurrying upstairs to pack for my trip back to Atlanta so I won't worry him. I gather my cosmetics from the upstairs bathroom, and pull the faded green spread up over the bed, knowing John and I will be the next to sleep in it, so no need to change the sheets. Poppa and Tippy walk me out to the car despite my urging Poppa to stay put. I worry about his getting back up the porch steps, but I dare not say so. Instead, I back the car around slowly until I'm sure he has managed, and then I wave goodbye.

Six months pass, and the long-distance commute between Denver and Atlanta adds a new dimension to my marriage. I like the balancing act John and I work out, dividing our time between two cities although I am flying back to Denver more often than John is flying to Atlanta. The advantage to this is that he often makes dinner reservations at our favorite French restaurant for the nights I arrive in town.

"You've brought me here more often since I left than the whole time I lived in Denver," I tease as we enjoy escargot and a glass of wine.

He does not seem in a joking mood.

"I've asked Brian to start looking for a new partner," he says. "I've decided I'll move back to the farm permanently as soon as I can."

I am flabbergasted. I know our young son-in-law will do fine with the practice, but John's decision seems so sudden.

"I think I can work out a part-time practice with the urologist in Rabun County," John adds, with a little uncertainly in his voice. "Pop's health is deteriorating. I want to get on with making plans for the farm and for what we can do there."

I always knew our commute was temporary, but his decision causes me to face questions I'd been avoiding. "How are we going to work the finances?" I finally ask. "And what about your fishing and golfing buddies? What social life is there in Tiger?"

"Well, there's mostly Pop and Coach," John replies with a laugh, referring to Coach Arvel Holmes, the retired high school football coach who has been Poppa's right hand at the farm for more than twenty years. "I'm sure we'll meet some other empty nesters like us in the community," John continues, "and I'm not suggesting *you* move to Tiger full time. Not yet, anyhow." It is the "not yet" that bothers me. I have never lived in a small town, and I'm not sure I want to.

"I've been thinking about what we could grow on the farm that would be interesting and help us make ends meet. I think I'll try starting a vineyard."

"Muscadine grapes or Concords?" I ask.

"No. Fine European wine grapes—*vinifera*."

I laugh out loud, but he looks quite serious.

Only then do I learn that since I'd moved from Denver, John has spent his time reading up on viticulture, the growing of fine wines. He has even gone so far as to talk with vineyard experts.

"On my last trip to the farm from Atlanta," he confesses, "I stopped at Habersham Vineyards and Winery. You've seen the sign—it's about forty miles south of Tiger."

"Habersham Winery makes sweet wines," I reply.

"Yes, mostly," John admits, "but the Habersham owner is also the first to plant *vinifera* grapes in Georgia, and it seems they've done all right."

When he stopped at Habersham, he tells me, he met a winemaker who'd studied in California. He suggested John talk with Dennis Horton, a Virginia winery owner, about planting Norton grapes. "Norton is a native American grape that thrives in the southeast and makes a dry red wine," John tells me, clearly excited.

A vineyard sounds pie-in-the-sky to me. "Don't wine grapes like dry climes, like the Napa Valley?" I ask. "And Horton's Norton—is this guy for real?" Maddeningly enough, John just smiles and nods. I persist. "You are seriously telling me that you want to grow wine grapes in the Bible belt? The land of known teetotalers? And you're going to plant them in Georgia's northernmost mountain county, one of the wettest counties in the whole country—how risky can we be, John?"

My husband is clearly not going to be deterred. He is all pumped up to pay this Dennis Horton a visit as soon as possible. I immediately envision my weekends devoted to digging, planting, nursing bug bites, and eating take-out barbecue from Oinkers just down the highway. There will be no time for boating on the nearby lakes, hiking and picking wildflowers, growing herbs—things about weekend farm and mountain life that appeal to me.

"If it's such a great idea to grow wine grapes this far north in Georgia, why isn't anybody else doing it?" I ask.

John doesn't flinch. "This was moonshine country. Nobody thought of it."

Then he tells me a funny story from his childhood, about two deacons in the Baptist church who routinely took a taxi to the liquor store because some church member might recognize their cars parked at such a place. He swears it is true.

John begins coming to Georgia more frequently. Although I remain skeptical about how a conservative rural community will accept wine growing, John doggedly works out a schedule with our surgeon son-in-law to spend every other month at the farm planning for his grand vineyard-to-be. When he arrives in Atlanta on a Friday, I sometimes try to interest him in a concert at the symphony hall across the street from my apartment—he's a classical music lover (or he always was before)—but to no avail. I also try luring him to one of the lively city restaurants I've discovered.

"You have to see Virginia Highlands," I plead. "It's a funky in-town area that reminds me of Washington Park in Denver. We'll eat at Indigo if it's not too crowded—you'll love the blackened mahi-mahi."

"What if we stop at that take-out down Peachtree Street that you told me about? We could take pasta salads with us to the farm," he counters, seeing that as a big concession because he's never been much of a pasta fan.

"You know," I continue, "you haven't even seen my favorite two parks—"

"What if I just buy you a Starbucks on the way out?" John offers. He sits down to read the *Journal-Constitution* sports pages. "I thought you'd be ready to go."

It doesn't matter what glorious things I try in order to entice John to spend just one Friday evening in the city. Each time he comes to Atlanta, it is clear he can't wait to hit the road to Tiger. I moan regularly about his rush to the country—there are plays I want to see, galleries I want to explore with him. But, in the end, I have to admire his single-mindedness about getting on with figuring out our new life-to-be at the farm. Weekend after weekend, I reluctantly throw my week's laundry, my reading folder, jeans, and hair dryer in a bag, and we head out for Tiger—not exactly the most cosmopolitan Friday evenings.

2

Horton's Norton and the Latte Crowd

When he isn't reading about Norton, John is rattling off the names of other weird wine grapes he's heard are suitable for cultivating in the southeast: Tannat and Touriga Nacional, for example. I can't understand what has come over my husband. He is usually the model of practicality. I know John's wine-growing dreams don't include growing Pinot Noir, the delicate grape our connoisseur friends think is cultivated in heaven, but *surely* we could start with a respectable grape like Merlot rather than a bizarre American grape!

"We've got to carve out time to go to Virginia and learn about Horton's Norton," he declares one morning over a bowl of cereal. "Gordonsville is near Charlottesville. It's only a day's drive."

"What's the 'we' stuff?" I reply, throwing up my hands. "How about listening to my ideas rather than fixating on Horton's Norton?"

"Go ahead," John nods his head impatiently.

I know his two-minute-warning look all too well so I talk fast. "Let's reconsider planting orchards on the farm. Peaches, apples, pears."

"Granddaddy already tried that, and it didn't work out. We've talked about this," John says. Then he continues,

"Peaches, for example, are much more vulnerable up here to late frost than grapes are."

I doubt my husband really knows that for sure, but I refrain from saying so. I try a delaying tactic. "Why don't we take a little time to travel to the villages of Bordeaux first, and see how the small vineyards work?" I dare not suggest a California trip. John fancies our Tiger vineyards will resemble the vineyards that thrive in the small villages of France, vineyards with distinctly different climate and soils than those on the west coast—more similar to the mountains of North Georgia, he believes. We have been to Paris, but we've never spent any significant time in the Bordeaux area. We have no idea how difficult it might be to make a small vineyard profitable. A trip could bring a dose of reality to my husband.

John ignores my suggestion and repeats the same old thing he's been saying for days: "The key to a successful vineyard in the Southeast is choosing grape varieties that will tolerate the humidity and love the soils and the seasons of the ancient Blue Ridge."

"Sounds like farm talk, not wine talk," I scoff.

I imagine peddling baskets of Norton at the farmers' market alongside Scuppernongs—slippery sweet grapes that make my skin crawl. One thing I know for sure: my ideal life as a weekend farm dweller does not include selling grapes out of the back of a pick-up.

"Then I want to see and taste Horton's Norton for myself," I say with a sigh.

As luck would have it, the only week John can arrange a visit with Dennis and Sharon Horton is when I am in the middle of writing a special series of editorials at the newspaper. It is an assignment I had coveted, and I didn't have time to sleep, much less travel to Virginia. At first, it seems the fates have bought me some time; the trip can be delayed and maybe John will reconsider orchards. But I am wrong. John is determined to forge ahead on his vineyard venture. Eager to meet the man he believes knows the most about growing wine grapes in the South, he makes plans to visit him right away. Once he arrives at Horton Vineyards, he calls me every day to tell me about the new and wondrous things he's learned about grape growing.

"But what about the grape *market*?" I ask.

"That's a silly question," he replies without explaining why it is silly to wonder how we can make a living, pay for rejuvenating one hundred acres of farmland, and build a new home. I am working on a deadline at the office, and the call is too short for the marketing conversation. Still, I secretly hope John's visit to Horton's vineyard may yet give him pause about the whole undertaking. He admits though that he's learned already that tending a vineyard is a lot more work than he ever imagined. When he returns from Virginia, I promise to get off work early enough for us to have dinner together at the farm. (I know Poppa is going to church supper with a cousin that evening.) "I'm going to try to beat the Friday evening traffic," I pledge, when we talk on the phone. "I made some chicken tortillas and a salad so we can eat there."

I had bought some special tulip and iris bulbs too, at a nursery near my city condo. I take the box of bulbs to the car as soon as I hang up so I won't forget them. Adding a few aesthetic touches to the old farm that offers so many possibilities for such is high on my agenda, though certainly not on my husband's.

On the drive to Tiger the next day, I am feeling skeptical and downright worried about this crazy venture. But as soon as I arrive, John meets me at the car to help me take things inside. He is absolutely ebullient, like a kid immersed in a new science project. I hadn't seen him looking this happy since he returned from his last fishing trip with a five-pound brown trout, and I silently promise to suspend my doubts about the project, if only for this evening. We set the table together; I dish out the salad and the tortillas, then light some candles I discover in a kitchen drawer and we sit down to eat.

John barely notices the candles or the cloth napkins I've gotten out. "I wish you could see how vibrant Dennis's Norton vines are," he says immediately, even before picking up his fork. "The grapes he recommends I plant are unusual for sure, but I can tell he knows what will produce quality fruit in the Southeast." I note he is already on a first name basis with his new vintner friend. He continues, "And the best news is we can pick up Norton cuttings for free and root them from scratch."

I grimace, my fork freezing midway to my mouth. The best news in my mind would be a declaration that he had decided to plant apple orchards. Remembering my promise to myself, I bite my tongue.

"Did the Hortons root their own Norton vines?" I ask after finishing my bite of salad.

"No," John replies, "but it can be done. They're encouraging me to try it."

"What kind of wine does this strange Norton grape make?" I feel my resolve to see the merits of the weird American varietal begin to evaporate.

"I'll get Coach to help me pot the cuttings and find a greenhouse this winter to start them in," John replies, ignoring my question. And then, as if on their own accord, my true thoughts burst forth.

"If we're going to have a vineyard, I'd really, *really* like to grow *fine* wine grapes. Otherwise we might as well make blueberry wine in a jug!"

"Look," John says, sounding exasperated, "if you want to produce grapes that make fine wine, you've got to grow grapes that make fine fruit in this humid climate. As Dennis puts it, 'Not all wine grapes are created equal,' and that's especially true for Southern wine growers. Dennis suggests some other reds besides Norton—all of them are European, you'll be happy to know. For whites, he says we ought to try Viognier instead of Chardonnay, though."

I burst forth with all of the questions I'd been wondering about, and not in a pleasant tone of voice.

"So now you want to plant other strange grapes besides Norton," I moan. "Let's get real—what is green-housing grape plants, buying trellises and wires and sprays and vineyard equipment going to cost, and how we were going to pay for all of it?" I finally wind down with, "So are you honestly telling me these...these little *sticks* you plan to pick up are going to turn into grapes we can sell to wineries, not just the corner grocery?"

John nods. He seems utterly unfazed by my tirade.

"Whoever heard of Norton?" I say sarcastically, trying to goad him out of silence.

"Thomas Jefferson, that's who," John shoots back. He is suddenly loquacious. "The grape is associated with the Monticello vineyards. Well, it probably wasn't cultivated at Monticello until after Jefferson's death. It was first grown in the 1820s in Richmond by a doctor named Daniel Norton, and some of the vines were sent to Jefferson's grandson, who was running the Monticello vineyards. Nobody knows for sure if he planted them. Still, Jefferson was the one who urged his gentleman farmer friends to grow American grapes after his efforts to cultivate French grapes failed—"

"Is Norton sweet?" I want to cut to the chase.

John is annoyed. "No. Norton isn't anything like scuppernong or muscadine—it makes a full-bodied dry wine and it's in a class by itself, *vitus aestavalis*."

"And *vitus veritas* to you," I say trying to sound like a wine snob. "What about Chardonnay or Merlot—wouldn't those be a smarter choice in the long run?" *Not to mention*, I thought, *something I won't be embarrassed to tell our friends about*.

"Dennis has studied this," my husband says, exasperated. "He's looked at which grapes actually yield quality fruit in the Southeast. And, yes, he has some Chardonnay, Cabernet Sauvignon, and Merlot. But others, like Cabernet Franc, grow better in our humid conditions. Here, I want you to taste this," he says, pulling out a bottle of Horton's Norton.

I fight the urge to ask if it comes with *Cat in the Hat.*

I want to taste the Norton in the right setting...and in a better frame of mind. I take a deep, cleansing breath. "Why don't we take the bottle to Glen Ella and have dinner tomorrow night?" I suggest. "I'll fix Poppa his early supper, and he'll want to watch the Braves game." Pockets of prohibition still dot the rural South; one of my favorite country chic inns, Glen Ella Springs, allows guests to bring their own bottles to the dining room since it is located in a county that won't grant a license to sell alcohol.

"Maybe," John replies.

He puts down the bottle and eats another bite of salad. We clink our glasses of sweet iced tea together, the Southern toast, of course.

The next morning I want to resume the wine growing conversation with my husband, but he rushes out to fix a tractor that is giving him some grief, so I decide to get my bulbs planted. Coach stops by just as I start to get down to work to tell me I should be wearing a hat in the sun. The seventy-year-old former high school football coach, dressed in his one-piece work overalls and stained hat, has lately taken on the role of my instructor in country ways.

"Also, those lilies you planted at the corner of the barn last weekend are gonna keep me from mowing up close. Could mean a lot of unnecessary hand trimming."

He says this with a twinkle in his eye, but I recognize it as a signal that he might "accidentally" run my new lilies over with the tractor. Ever since I started spending time at Tiger, he makes a point of telling me what John wants him to do. If I add any extra task, he responds that he will check with John about it.

"The blueberry bushes aren't close to the barn," I counter. "Why don't you mow around them and I'll trim around my new lilies?"

"I'll talk to John about it. He wants me to get the dirt road by the barn scraped before the rain comes in tomorrow." He points to the field behind the barn, dotted with huge round hay bales against the mountain backdrop, the old tractor John is fixing poised in front of them. To my eye the scene is a Norman Rockwell painting and the narrow road is a fine part of it. "It's rutted out in several places," Coach continues. I know he'll just widen the road and make it less like the scenic lane I want it to be.

His lecture about my new lilies being trouble is so predictable I have to smile.

Coach smiles back. "Don't you fret about the mowing so," he drawls. "I stand on that hill over there by the chicken house every morning and I pretend this place is mine. I care for it like it's mine. The Colonel's always known that."

"Hey, why are you working on a Saturday?" I ask, suddenly recalling that his regimen calls for "weekends off—period."

"Don't you know it's time for me to lay the farm by?"

"Do what?" I ask, wondering if "laying by" means he is calling it quits.

"When harvest is over and you see the last hay bales of summer, it's purty nigh time to get things ready for another season. Might as well cut down the okra and corn stalks and start laying the farm by for winter," he says.

I feel relieved that Coach is talking about another season. He has worked for Poppa for the last twelve years. John couldn't do without him, especially now. I take up my trowel and begin to dig a hole for one of my tulip bulbs.

"Now, that's good dirt," Coach says pointing to the earthworms I am trying to avoid. "You could sell those for fishing bait down at Alley's store."

Everybody in the Ezzard family believes Alley's is *the* place to go for a fishing license, a bucket of crickets, canned sardines, crackers, wedges of red hoop cheese, and Moon Pies. Never in my wildest dreams, though, did I think anybody would suggest this city girl should go sell worms—at Alley's or anywhere else. Coach is teasing, but it's bad timing given my recent misgivings about farm life.

"What do you think about John's vineyard plans?" I ask, changing the subject to our common interest in the vineyards-to-be.

"Don't matter what I think," he says with a chuckle. "He's an Ezzard and he's as stubborn as any of 'em. John's already got me looking for a source for his trellis wires," he adds. "Metal posts, too, and they're gonna cost plenty." He shakes his head. "Did John tell you he's going to drive up to a place in Pennsylvania to pick up some specialized equipment?"

As he turns in the direction of the barn, he is still chuckling and shaking his head. I can tell Coach is as excited as John about the wine grape challenge. I am beginning to feel like the last person on the beach when the tide comes in sweeping away all moorings. I dig a hole for my next bulb.

This is all happening so fast! I dig another hole. We've never even talked about how we can sell grapes! And I have no idea what a harvest of wine grapes grown in North Georgia would bring, cash-wise. I put down my trowel and gaze out on the pond where a blue heron is alighting on the willows lining its edge. Saving the family farm sounds romantic enough in theory, but where is the money going to come from to do it?

John finally comes in from working on Poppa's tractor. I have long since finished planting my bulbs and am relaxing in the shade on the porch while I have a moment to catch up on my reading.

"Do you want me to make dinner reservations at Glen Ella?" I ask.

"Is Poppa up from his nap?"

"He is, and he is leaving soon."

"Then I really need to take him over to my vineyard site while he's feeling rested. I'd settle for a Dairy Queen hot dog, though," he adds, a bit sheepishly.

I do not respond. If a hot dog at the Dairy Queen is to be my Saturday night dinner, canned pork and beans on the back porch are surely just around the corner.

A few hours later, as twilight tiptoes in, John and I sit in the front porch rocking chairs. "How does Poppa feel about the wine grapes?" I ask, knowing my father-in-law does not drink. John chuckles.

"He's just happy we're going to keep the farm cultivated," he says. "He knows Coach and I are taking care of the sweet corn and the berries." The rolling hills around us are slowly fading into a single rippling line against the night sky. Our neighbor has just finished "tedding" the hayfields across the road, a process of fluffing up the mown hay before baling it. The sweet fresh smells and the twilight haze rising from the fields, a full moon peeking over the misty backdrop as if it were a curtain for a stage performance, make me feel as if I'm stepping into the first act of an exciting drama, despite the chaos of our changing lives.

"Why don't we open the Horton wine now?" I suggest, having decided a candlelight occasion isn't to be. "I'll get some cheese and fruit out of the refrigerator."

John agrees. "Let's let it breathe for about a half hour though," he says, as I carry a small plate of strawberries and a wedge of our favorite South Carolina Clemson blue cheese to the porch.

"Remind me why Jefferson wasn't able to grow French grapes," I say, settling back in my rocking chair as we wait for the wine to open up.

I already know that European wine grapes—*vinifera*—must be grafted onto American rootstock to survive.

"Jefferson didn't know about phylloxera," John explains. "After his death, the mite that got into the soil in America and kept his imported vines from maturing also wiped out vineyards in Europe."

John goes on to explain the scientific details of it, but the story is essentially this: One day, a smart Frenchman began to wonder why the native American grapes hadn't been devastated by phylloxera. The American grapes obviously had a natural resistance to it. Eventually, a group of French wine growers came up with the idea to graft the European *vinifera* onto American rootstock (such as Concords and other native grapes), a practice that continues today. Some growers graft their own, but most do what we're doing and buy the grafted *vinifera* from special nurseries.

John pours two glasses of the dark, plum-colored wine. I expect something akin to muscadine, but it is a surprisingly dry wine with flavors of blackberries and cherries as well as subtle hints of tobacco and chocolate. It is the finish, though, the lingering spiciness that is its most notable characteristic. The taste is unexpected—unbidden memories of John's grandmother and her berry cobblers always tinged with nutmeg and spices come to mind. Finally, I nod approvingly. "A native grape just might work," I say slowly, eyeing the attractive Norton label. "But who's going to buy a wine they never heard of?"

"Who's talking about selling *wine*?" John smiles, clearly pleased by my reaction. "We'll grow the grapes at very little expense and sell them to wineries. I know you're worried about finances. But don't forget—I'll get something substantial for my Denver practice when I leave, and I intend to practice medicine here part-time. With your income, too, we should be fine. And building a house on the farm shouldn't cost us more than we'll make when we sell our home in Denver."

I take another sip of Norton. "To a risk worth taking," I reply, holding up my glass and giving him a hug.

John has one more week at the farm before heading back to Denver to catch up on his medical practice, but word travels fast in a small town. Old timers he runs into at the local hardware store have already heard from Coach and other farmers about the planned vineyard. Lewis Reeves, the second generation owner of three Reeves stores in Clayton—stores that include everything from upscale furniture to feed, seed, and construction materials—slaps John on the back to welcome him home, saying he thinks John's vineyard idea might be "worth a try."

Other locals are more skeptical.

"Wait just a minute now, John, what's wrong with muscadines?" asks Bob Ramey, a local service station owner who was in elementary school with him. Others remind my husband that Grandpa Arrendale had given up on orchards years ago when consecutive spring freezes wiped out his apple business. But there are still apple orchards thriving in Rabun County, so maybe Grandpa Arrendale just reacted to an unfortunate series of spring frosts. John laughs off their comments, and I don't say a word, thinking it is too hard for old timers to grant much credence to wine grapes since they have never been cultivated in the area before. I find it curious that so many people in the community have already heard of our plans; knowing my neighbors' business isn't something I am accustomed to. In my city condo I know the names of only two couples on my floor. In Tiger it soon becomes apparent that any new undertaking on the Ezzard farm—even one old-timers clearly view as a harebrained idea—is going to attract plenty of interest. I suspect that's how our across-the-road neighbor, Mike Dixon, a farmer and one of our county commissioners, views John's vineyard dream, but he never says so, instead offering to loan John heavy equipment or help however he can. One evening, noting how much the Colonel's farm vehicles have deteriorated, Mike advises John that he needs a new bushog.

"A *what?*" I ask John later, when we are alone. We had both stood and talked to Mike for a good half hour when he pulled his tractor up in front of the old creamery building, but I was too embarrassed to let Mike know I had no idea what a bushog is.

A bushog, I learn from John, is a piece of farm equipment for clearing land, weeds, and brush. A new one would cost us thousands. I had a feeling even a good used bushog means my plan to hire a landscaper to put in a row of flowering trees and shrubs along the gravel road to the barn will quickly fall by the wayside. This is a project we had discussed the weekend before John first went to Virginia; he and I talked about our immediate needs at the farm over a quick dinner at my Atlanta apartment. John hates lists, but I'd made one anyhow, so he jotted down a few things too, mostly equipment. My list included beautifying the farm with flowering trees, shrubs and lilies, a matter, it turned out, on which we disagreed. "That's putting the cart before the horse," John said. "We need to buy some basic equipment and get the vines planted first."

We agreed to disagree at the time, but we found common ground in fixing up the barn—it is in terrible shape, its dilapidated condition resembling a piece of folk art with funny shaped rusty metal patches nailed on worn wood to keep it from leaking. The old barn and its magnificent silo are the entry to the farm and rejuvenating the barn is important to both of us—a symbol that the land will continue to be a working farm.

As it turns out, John passes on the bushog. Acknowledging that Mike is right about upgrading, he nevertheless declares that a good farm truck is his immediate priority. He is tired of depending on Coach's truck to haul trellis wires and other vineyard equipment. I am relieved at his decision, and pleased too, because I envision a farm truck as an essential part of our country image, like a pair of jeans with a slightly worn but snappy look. "Country cool," you might say.

"Have you seen the new Toyota Tundra?" I ask John. "In silver or maybe forest green—"

"Surely you don't think I'm going to buy one of those latte crowd trucks?" he says with a note of distain in his voice.

"What do you mean, *latte truck*?" I know for a fact that my husband, who is not a coffee drinker, has never even tasted a latte. But even when we were living in the city, John kept a rusty old car or truck for going fishing. He has never bought a brand new car; it's a farm boy trait that never left him.

"I don't want one of those 'show' trucks city folks drive, with a bed barely big enough for a bushel of corn," he says. "I'm looking for a long bed for hauling. You can't find any new trucks designed for real farming," he adds.

I privately hope he won't find an old one either, but that very afternoon John's brother Henry tells him about a friend who wants to sell a 1985 Ford truck. The next day, John drives up to the rock house in one of the ugliest vehicles I've ever seen.

"It's perfect for hauling trellis posts and fishing poles," he exclaims.

All I can do is nod. When I drive the rusty white thing for the first time, I discover the needle on the automatic gearshift is missing, so I have to count the clicks to get it into reverse. It has no radio and a heater fan that sounds like a helicopter. I truly hate it and try to avoid driving it, but Tippy follows it around the farm dutifully, knowing John is nearby. She is as attached to John as she is to Poppa even though I am the one who feeds her when Poppa can't. When John drives his old truck to town for the first time, the locals nod approvingly at him as if he's never left home at all.

After the arrival of "truck tacky," as I name it, I can hardly wait for John's departure. I am usually sad to see him leave for Denver, it's true, but this time, I am glad. I plan to exercise my ridiculed "latte snob" instincts freely in his absence. And I fully intend to get Coach's help.

Coach is never beyond lobbying me to persuade John to purchase equipment that *he* wants—on the pretense that he can do more "sprucin' up" around the farm. "Well, Maah-tha, I *could* make the grass along the roadside look a lot better if John would consider a new mower attachment...."

So the weekend after John goes back to Denver, I say to Coach, "I'll talk up some new mowing equipment if you'll talk up some new trees."

Coach's eyes light up. "Now that's the kind of horse tradin' I like."

I purchase some flowering cherry trees and arrange to have a couple of dogwoods moved from the woods to the farmhouse side of the creamery, the small cement block building on the side of the road that Poppa has neglected since his beloved wife Ruth died. Then I plant some holly bushes and add a climbing Carolina jasmine beside the creamery front door. I paint the door bright yellow so it will match the jasmine's yellow blossoms and have some new gravel brought in for the front of the building. The building itself needs a coat of paint, but that will have to wait. Coach—despite declaring that the transplanted dogwoods won't live—stays true to our newly formed alliance and promises to water the new trees and shrubs for me while I am in Atlanta.

My fix-up blitz also includes some new green-checked curtains in the farmhouse to replace the worn beige drapes and a fresh coat of paint in the downstairs bathroom. Poppa likes all of my fixing up, and he tells me the next weekend that one of his Rotary Club pals hollered to him across the grocery aisle with a comment about it. "That yellow door is the first sign I'd seen that things are a'changin' over at Ezzard's place," the old-timer told Poppa.

The total impact of my fix-up blitz gives me a rush of energy for my work at the paper as well—the feeling that obstacles to a worthy project can always be overcome. I can't wait to see the look on John's face when he returns. I might have to buy him his first latte.

The abundance of native hardwood on Tiger Mountain brings back memories of summer vacations I took during my childhood—my mother was fond of exclaiming over the diversity of the trees in the Blue Ridge Mountains although I was too young at the time to appreciate her observation. The week after the creamery makeover I write a column about the need for state mountain protection legislation, lest our blue ridges end up with roads cut into their ridgelines and resemble snaggle-toothed children. After the piece is published I receive a phone call from Dr. Bob Hatcher, an Emory University professor and part-time Tiger resident.

"Maggie and I loved your column," he says, "and we want you and your husband to come over for dinner. We're your Tiger neighbors."

We chat about Georgia's weak environmental laws, and I learn that Hatcher not only is passionate about preservation of our mountain environment but also has written books on family planning—another one of John's and my causes—that have been translated into several languages and distributed though the United Nations to developing countries.

"John is in Denver," I say with much regret, but at Maggie's insistence, I agree to go over for dinner anyhow.

At the Hatchers' dinner party, I find some soul mates: Tiger neighbors who share my interest in food and wine, hiking and gardening. There is hardly anyone in Tiger who isn't growing tomatoes, lettuces, and cucumbers. John grew sweet corn and okra in our backyard even in Denver. And I envy the Hatchers' well-groomed gardens and the charming home that Maggie, an artist and interior decorator, has designed. Its wrap-around porch looks out on two large ponds and rolling apple orchards. Tiger Mountain rises in the distance, its tumbling ridges convincing me for the first time that John's theory about a crouched tiger profile really could be the genesis of its name.

Sitting in a rocking chair on Hatchers' porch after dinner, I feel wonderfully at home. "My mother introduced me to the biodiversity of these mountains when we came up on vacations," I commented, "but I didn't pay serious attention at the time. I wish I had."

Other guests chime in to describe their favorite native trees—sycamore, tulip popular, red oak, sugar maple, hickory.

"Didn't you write a column about a hike over Tiger Mountain with a friend who lives on the other side?" Hatcher asks.

"Yes," I reply, "John's granddad always said you should get to know your neighbor on the other side of the mountain. There's no trail, you know, but I bushwhacked right over the top with Pierce Cline, an avid hiker, who owns a cabin on the other side of the mountain."

"There were wild boars and mountain lions out there in John's granddad's day," says Maggie, bringing a tray of scrumptious desserts and coffee to the porch.

The soft evening air and silhouette of the mountain furnish a romantic backdrop for her gracious entertaining. I feel as if I have never left the South I knew as a child. As I drive home that evening, I can hardly wait to telephone John and tell him what interesting people I've met. The dinnertime discussion is still on my mind when I enter the small living and dining area of the rock farmhouse. Both rooms are paneled in chestnut. I feel as if I am really seeing the interesting knotty wood for the first time.

"Poppa, does chestnut always have such intricate patterns in the grain?" I ask the next morning at breakfast.

"This is wormy chestnut," Poppa explains. "It's a sad reminder of the tree's demise."

He goes on to recount that the American chestnut, thanks to an Asian bark fungus, disappeared from most Appalachian forests in the mid-1900s. Worms bored into them even before the giant trees began to fall. The wood was still sturdy and the wormy wood with its intricate patterns became sought after for homes and buildings. As he describes the demise of the mighty American chestnuts, I can tell he is still mourning the disappearance of "the forest giant" as he calls the near-extinct tree. (Tiny chestnut trees sprout in the forest but die after a few years.)

"I had no idea that this paneling is so rare."

"It is. The Chinese chestnuts I planted beyond the barn are resistant to that fungus, but they're not as large or nearly as majestic," he says, shaking his head to underscore the loss.

I had already confided to Poppa that I'd been selected to be part of a five-newspaper project to hike the entire 2000-mile Appalachian Trail in relay fashion this spring, with all five newspapers publishing "Appalachian Adventure,"[1] our stories from the trail, as a weekly series, later compiled and published as a book by the same name. I'd been a casual hiker and had never backpacked, but the project editor wanted all levels of expertise and a range of ages. I applied, and, to my astonishment, was chosen. Poppa had laughed when I told him I was getting in shape by hiking the five-mile loop around Stone Mountain in Atlanta on weekday evenings.

---

[1] Elizabeth Lee, ed., *Appalachian Adventure* (Marietta: Lonstreet Press, 1999).

"You're not training with that pack empty now, are you, girl?" he inquired.

"Nope," I respond proudly. "I'm stuffing it with a camp stove and plenty of gear, just to see how it feels."

I hadn't told John yet. I felt guilty about being gone for ten days during spring planting time. I break it to him that evening, over the phone, with some trepidation.

"That's terrific," he says. "You'll have a chance to do the kind of outdoors writing you love, and don't worry about the vines. You can help me through the first week of May. I'll be finished with spring planting by the time you leave."

He is tickled that two of our three grown children, Lisa and John Jr., will be able to join me on segments of the trail. I feel tremendously relieved.

Meanwhile, as autumn turns to winter, a November ice storm hits Georgia and spring backpacking seems far away. John's and my commuting schedules become even more hectic during the Thanksgiving holiday as we try to squeeze in time with family and friends in both Colorado and Georgia. I still worry privately about the grape-growing venture while John gets more and more excited about it. Old friends we chat with in Denver are curious about our new life and admire our risk taking. John keeps answering the same questions. ("How did you know what kinds of grapes to plant?" "You don't have a crew to help you?" "How is Martha's life in a city high rise?" "Aren't you coming back out for a few weeks to ski?") John genuinely enjoys sharing his vineyard adventure stories while listening to our friends' questions. Witnessing their fascination and curiosity make me feel newly grateful about this fresh chapter of our lives.

When December comes and we decide to stay in Georgia for Christmas, I miss the neighborhood parties and concerts we've grown accustomed to attending in Denver. Still, I am stunned by the natural beauty of my first Georgia mountain Christmas season. On weekends at the farm I pick holly and winter greens; I decorate the mantle with magnolia leaves and nandina berries, and I discover mistletoe in the woods. The parasitic plants are so high on the trees that I have to get John to bring a ladder and hold it for me in the back of the hated white pick-up so I can climb up and gather it. It is the first time I appreciate the ugliest truck in the world.

It snows one evening just before Christmas, and the farm is a wonderland. Still, I grumble about having to work and travel on the icy roads to Atlanta. I'd volunteered to work through the holidays since some of my editorial board colleagues have young children and need time off worse than I. The farm seems all too quiet; I miss the city holiday bustle, our Denver friends, and our traditional holiday parties and concerts.

"Why in the world can't we fix this chimney so we can have a real fire?" I complain to John one evening. "I mean, what's an Appalachian Christmas for?"

The rock fireplace in the small farmhouse is perfect for the size of the room, but I couldn't remember ever seeing a fire in it.

John gets down on his knees and peers up the chimney in a half-hearted effort to see what the problem with it might be. I know it isn't a project he'll tackle any time soon.

"You know, I was just thinking today that we should put a gas fireplace in our new home," he jokes, knowing how much I love the smell of crackling logs and trying to tease me out of my bad mood.

I ignore his comments and wrap myself in a Grandma Tallulah-crocheted afghan that I found in an upstairs bedroom, once her sewing room. Rummaging earlier through the farmhouse bookshelves, I came across a copy of *Christmas in Georgia*,[2] an old favorite written by Celestine Sibley, now my *Atlanta Journal-Constitution* colleague. I feel fortunate to have talked with her from time to time, even solicited a little writing advice. The characters in her book remind me to appreciate human imperfection; they are so real, so Southern, so lovable, so flawed.

John goes to bed early, and I snuggle down in his favorite easy chair, happy to stay up a while longer to reread Celestine's work. The old afghan is soft and cozy, and I felt toasty warm despite the lack of a fire. I notice the crocheted afghan has one square in the middle of it—charming for sure—made of leftover yarns that don't match the colors in the rest of the handmade blanket.

I realize in that moment that I don't want to be like that odd square.

I want to feel at home in Tiger.

---

[2] Celestine Sibley, *Christmas in Georgia* (Garden City, NY: Doubleday, 1964).

3

How Do You Spell *Tannat*?

Right after Christmas, John begins talking about the kinds of grapes he wants to plant, except for the American Norton, all European *vinifera*: Cabernet Franc, Malbec, Touriga Nacional and Tannat.

On a ski trip to Colorado, some friends who love wines, Katie and Alan Fox, ask gently if John is going to plant any Chardonnay or Merlot. "How do you spell *Tannat*, John?" asks Alan, whose wine cellar has always been one to envy. The question simply reinforces my skepticism about the offbeat varieties John has selected.

"You're not the first one to ask that," John replies with a chuckle. "Chardonnay just needs a longer, hotter growing season than we have in North Georgia, and Dennis Horton, who studied which grapes produce quality fruit in the southeast, advised me to grow Viognier as my primary white wine grape. It's more suitable for our climate and soils and doesn't bud out too early because we'll have to worry some about late spring frost in North Georgia. Merlot isn't one of the reds I've chosen for some of those same reasons, but some folks say it would do just fine at our location. Even Cabernet Sauvignon, which Dennis grows, isn't as adaptable to the southern clime as Tannat, a hearty grape from southwest France."

"It's all about *terrior*," I add, testing one of my new wine terms. *Terroir* is a French term that means the soils, rocks, terrain, climate, even the culture of the locale. Wine aficionados who have never lifted a hoe in the vineyard like to throw the word around. After fighting beetles and weeds, enduring broken fingernails and blisters on my hands from wielding a post hole digger to help John put in trellis posts, I figure I am overqualified to use it. I soon decide the term isn't snobby at all because understanding its true meaning is basic to cultivating fine wine grapes. My favorite definition is by Hugh Johnson, a world-renowned wine expert and author of *World Atlas of Wine*[3] and other books, who wrote in his introduction to James Wilson's book *Terrior*, "[Terroir is] the whole ecology of the vineyard: every aspect of its surroundings, from bedrock to late frosts and autumn mists, not excluding the way the vineyard is tended, not even the soul of the vigneron.[4]

My vigneron—John, of course—knows the soils of our farm from his first barefoot steps as a toddler in the family garden. He knows the feel of dirt between his fingers, the gravelly, flinty texture—sometimes crumbly, sometimes lying on top of a slick, tightly packed layer of red clay making red and brown streaks on his hands and arms. And he surmised when he started thinking of growing wine grapes on the slopes of Tiger Mountain that because the Appalachians are some of

---

[3] Hugh Johnson, *World Atlas of Wine* (Berkeley: University of California Press, 1999).

[4] Jame E. Wilson, *Terroir* (Berkeley: University of California Press, 1998) 4.

the oldest mountains in the world, that the soils and rocks could be more like those of the Bordeaux region of France than the soils of the drier and hotter Napa Valley. In this Blue Ridge Mountain region known for blackberries, raspberries, and blueberries, why wouldn't the berries of wine grape clusters also thrive and reflect the unique flavors of the fruits produced here for centuries past?

"If you want to know where fine wines are made," John says, referring to the advice of many an expert, "don't turn to the bottle label; look at what's beneath the earth where they grow."

The winter after his first visit to Horton Vineyards in Virginia, John decides to take Coach with him to pick up Norton cuttings that Dennis and Sharon offered. His plan is to root them and nurse them through the winter months in a greenhouse, possibly the one at the Rabun County High School, which is run by the agriculture teacher, a family friend.

The Hortons had purchased their plants from a nursery, but Sharon—who manages the approximate hundred acres of vineyards—is convinced the American grape will grow from cuttings and encourages John to try it. Once again, John calls me every day with some bit of news about his vineyard-to-be while visiting the Hortons. On this trip, he is not only planning for his Norton vines but also ordering through Sharon the other types of grapes he wants to put in. When he shares his selections with me over the phone, I'm glad he can't see my expressions.

Cabernet Franc and Malbec I've at least heard of, but Touriga Nacional, Mourvedre, and Tannat are foreign to me. "For heaven's sake!" I say finally. "Who has ever heard of Tannat? And what kind of wine does it make?"

"It's musty and earthy and inky dark," John replies. "It comes from the Madiran in southwestern France, near the Pyrenees, and it's often used for blending, but it can make a good varietal wine—we'll see."

"Hmmm, earthy—so it has a nose like damp leaves on the farm," I tease. "I thought we were just growing grapes, but it *would* be fun to make wine if we had the money to get it started." I realize suddenly that I am the one dreaming. John brings me back to earth talking about his Norton "sticks."

"Don't be upset," he warns, "when you see these Norton cuttings Coach and I have collected. They are all a combination of old wood and new bud wood, but they look like plain old sticks." I have no idea what he means by old and new wood, but I can hardly wait to see them.

Each pruned cutting John and Coach select has a new shoot coming off the old wood from the previous year I soon learn. John looks carefully for cuttings of old wood with three buds on a new shoot, the new wood that has grown from it the previous season. The roots of a new vine will grow out of the old wood when the cutting is planted. When he gets home, he buys tubular pots, wide at the top, narrow and open at the bottom, about twelve inches deep. He and Coach pot the cuttings in a mixture that is two-fifths sand, one-fifth vermiculite, and two-fifths potting soil.

"How did you know to do that?" I ask when I see the funny looking pots the following weekend.

"Everybody who's ever farmed knows how to mix potting soil," he shrugs, knowing that description does not include me. John's local contacts come in handy in his search for a greenhouse to nurse the plants through the winter and early spring. Not only is Steve Cabe, the high school agriculture teacher, a longtime friend, but the school principal, Matt Arthur, stayed in the farmhouse when he was first hired before moving his family to Clayton. It is easy for John to convince both that students could learn a lot from overseeing native American grapes as they sprout in the school greenhouse.

I am never surprised but often annoyed with John's do-it-yourself penchant, but, in this case, it is to our advantage not to have to buy hundreds of new plants. We visit the greenhouse regularly, taking friends with us. One of my former high school classmates from Atlanta, Joyce Ringer, and her husband, Wayne, help us water the plants one weekend and seem so excited about rooting them from scratch that I begin to think this whole scheme might turn out better than I expect. Six weeks later, to John's chagrin, we discover only 45 percent of the 900 cuttings are still alive. John had left two buds beneath the soil and one above. He studies the dead plants and decides he planted them too deep, that some buds had smothered trying to break out beneath the surface of the little pots. He should have left two buds above the soil, he says. I wonder why he hadn't found that out before he planted but soon learn he is the pioneer in rooting Norton. He hadn't been able to discover anyone in the Midwest or the

Southeast—the two areas of the country where the native grape is cultivated—who had tried to root it from cuttings.

Nevertheless, John has enough survivors for five rows of Norton in our first vineyard, 360 plants. Helping him put them in the ground is strangely enjoyable to me, "deliciously dirty work" as I describe it when our children call to check on our planting progress. John and Coach dig most of the holes for the small plants. Then, I help haul buckets of water and pour a little in each hole before we put the plant in. Actually we place the long tapered plastic pots themselves in the ground and wish they were biodegradable. John teaches some of the students to hold each plant in place while he slits the sides of the pots so they slide off without disturbing the plant at all.

"Why such a tedious process?" I ask meekly.

"The roots are too fragile for us to pull or dump the plants out of the pots," John replies in an exasperated tone, as if I should know such a thing. Soon, there is a proud moment when a row is done to stand back and see the spindly plants neatly placed in the red crumbly dirt, which John informs me isn't clay like everyone thinks, but ancient degenerated granite from the mountain—"flinty soil" he describes it, in wine terms. "Flinty" is a positive characteristic in some wines, I read recently in a wine book, although I'm not sure I will recognize it when I come upon that characteristic in a wine. I resolve quietly to look for it or at least think about it in some of the Rhone reds we have in our cellar.

Soon, John and Coach are hard at it, toting heavy metal poles and wires to raise trellises, which Coach describes as "no job for sissies." The two of them construct the trellises, based on the ones John has learned about from Dennis Horton. He and Coach then carefully measure to allow twelve feet between each of the rows of vines. Coach invents a shortcut, using a pre-cut board rather than pulling out the tape measure over and over for spacing the rows and lining up the trellis posts. I get looped into helping pound posts in the ground—not something I might have envisioned doing a few years before from the forty-seventh floor of my Denver law office.

"It's way better conditioning than your LA Fitness class in Atlanta," John says with a smirk.

After an hour of hammering the wooden posts, my arms and shoulders ache. I console myself that I won't have to worry about the mid-life horror of flabby arms if I keep at it. Worry I do, though, about blisters on my hands, broken fingernails, bee stings, chigger bites. (Chiggers are miniscule insects whose larvae stay in the swollen red welts they make and are best defeated with an old-fashioned mountain remedy, a coat of clear fingernail polish that smothers them.) Coach instructs me that such blemishes are a "routine" part of my job. Some of my editorial board colleagues, who seem genuinely surprised that I'm not just sipping wine in a scenic mountain sunset on weekends, tease me about my farm girl scars. One of them even discovers a tick on the back of my neck on a Monday morning—and it isn't as if I hadn't taken a shower after a Sunday of farm work. John hee-haws when I tell him about it, "How many city slickers does it take to remove one measly tick?"

John's Cabernet Franc plants arrive in early April from a recommended New York nursery that specializes in *vinifera*, Hermann Amberg. The French grapes come with the expected American rootstock graft bulging out above the bare roots; John has just enough of them for five rows—our first European *vinifera*. (I love the Cabernet Franc plants from the moment I first see them; they exhibit near perfect indented leaves even when they are tiny, but John thinks the Norton plants he's rooted—scrawny, crooked sticks with puny leaves—are grand.) John creates the Cabernet Franc vineyard across the gravel road from the Norton, on a hillside sloping towards a small creek that comes from an underground spring on the mountain, a creek that once supplied water for Grandpa Arrendale's farmhouse. John later calls this vineyard "hell's half acre" because the slope, great for the grapes, is hell for his old tractor, light years behind the slick narrow vineyard tractors we covet in Napa magazine advertisements.

John is obviously pumped up about planting our first vines, but I still think of the whole thing as a hobby, an interesting diversion. What I am excited about, and a little anxious too, is my first backpacking adventure coming up the end of May, a five-newspaper hiking and writing project for which I feel lucky to be selected. Our daughter Lisa, a teacher, poet and—thankfully—a seasoned backpacker, will fly to Atlanta from California to join me for the first half of the carefully planned ten-day trek. I have already attended hike workshops with my newspaper colleagues and helped send off the first twosome, writer and photographer, in late March from the Appalachian Trail's southernmost point atop

Springer Mountain, only an hour from our farm. Reporters, photographers, and a few editors from the five newspapers gathered there in anticipation of the relay-style 2158-mile journey. Each writer has a different take—one looks for wild edibles; another depicts the hike with illustrations; one reporter plans to hike with his dog. My angle is a family one, mother-daughter and then mother-son conversations in the woods. I will trek eighty miles in the Virginia wilderness—forty-two miles with Lisa and thirty-eight miles with John Jr. The newspaper buys me a three-and-a-half-pound tent and I begin shopping at outdoors stores for pre-packaged camping foods. My chief aim is to keep my backpack under thirty-five pounds, which means almost all cosmetics except sun block will have to go.

Backpacking with two of our children John thought an absolutely grand opportunity. (I wished Shelly, our oldest, could have come too, but she was expecting a baby in a few months.) John, of course, could care less about hiking unless there's good fishing along the way. That much I know from dragging him along on casual but sometimes arduous hikes with friends over the years.

After Lisa and I hike five days, John picks up John Jr., who flies in from Colorado, to switch places with Lisa and complete the hike with me. Father and son drive to meet us at the halfway point of my assigned section of the hike, Steele's Tavern, Virginia, where the legendary Sugar Tree Inn is located. The rustic bed and breakfast is nestled in the trees on the edge of the Appalachian Trail, which winds through the rugged Thomas Jefferson National Forest. When Lisa and I emerge from the woods near the inn an hour earlier than planned, we are ecstatic to see John and her brother waiting for us. John Jr. starts laughing at our bedraggled state, but Lisa can hardly wait to tell him about our adventure, including running into a bear and getting lost the first night.

While the two of them are chatting, I give my husband an extra hug. I know I've been missing from the farm at a busy time. Nevertheless, he never complains once to me about his ten-hour days in the vineyard, constantly encouraging me in my hiking and writing challenge. I notice how suntanned his face and forearms are. I've always loved his large sinewy hands, but for decades, they had that hospital-pale scrubbed look. Now even his fingernails reflect the earth he's been working in, lined in color that will only fade with time. Suddenly, it seems, he is transformed from surgeon to ruddy farmer, fifth generation steward of the Arrendale-Ezzard farm. I silently wonder how I have missed the transformation. I know for sure it's the part of him to which I was first attracted. That seems like yesterday, even as I backpack with two of our grown children, one just out of Yale and the other in her first teaching job.

After fifteen meals of dried fruit and instant noodles, Lisa and I savor every morsel of the roast duck dinner at the Sugar Tree Inn in Steele's Tavern, located just five minutes from the Appalachian Trail. My husband adds an impressive Virginia red wine to complement the duck. During the meal, John tells Lisa and John Jr. about the ten rows of grapes he has put in and about the other varietals he plans to add. Our son asks about the unusual trellis system, one that is divided in the middle to provide for more air and sun in the vine canopy, thus warding off the mildews that plague grape growers in humid conditions. John sketches the structure of the trellises on a paper napkin. Indeed, a few months before, when I first heard the names of the two trellis systems he'd chosen, "Geneva Double Curtain" and "Open Lyre," I thought he was joking. Geneva Double Curtain sounds to me like a fancy window covering, and Open Lyre conjures up an image of a Victorian parlor instrument. The Open Lyre trellis, like the lyre itself, has five wires on each side attached to metal frames resembling small football goal posts. John describes it in detail to our son and daughter and explains that Sharon Horton weaves the new canes on the vines in and out of the wires in spring and ties them in place before thinning, with the help of vineyard labor, of course.

"What vineyard labor have you got, Dad?" John Jr. inquires.

"Oh, Coach and I and others," he replies, grinning across the dinner table at me. He explains that the Norton will grow on the simpler Double Curtain trellis with one wire on each side of the posts, like a double of the single wire trellises used in dry regions like Napa Valley, a much less labor intensive system for sure. "I've already named Norton 'the kudzu of grape vines,'" John says, "just looking at the way it grows, in all directions." Then, he laughs out loud, "It's very undisciplined—very American."

John announces that he will add another four or five rows of Norton next spring and wants me to visit the Hortons' vineyard in the winter with him to pick up more cuttings. I agree and can't wait to meet his mentors.

John Jr. and I set out in the rain on the second half of the late May backpacking adventure. Mother and son in the woods is a different experience from mother and daughter. For one thing, we carry more food and plan our daily mileage more carefully, rarely dawdling over the iridescent rhododendron blossoms as Lisa and I had done. It's a good thing, psychologically, for me to tackle the Priest Mountain, notably one of the Appalachian Trial's toughest climbs, with my son, who acts as if it's no big deal. By the time we reach the mountain's 4,031-foot summit, which takes hikers up 3,000 feet in just four miles, my aching muscles tell me it's a very big deal. When the two of us, wet through and through, emerge thirty-eight miles and four days later at Rockfish Gap, John is waiting once again at our planned meeting spot. He has taken Lisa to the airport and made another trip to the Hortons' winery in between, where he spent time with a favorite winemaker of Dennis's. While I hang out in a Holiday Inn (where the newspaper had made reservations and delivered a laptop for me), poring over my wrinkled, damp notes, to write for five hours and file my story, John drives our son back to D.C. to catch his flight to Colorado. He returns late, and we both decide to sleep in the next morning and head back to the farm around lunch. I suggest we stop that night at one of many historic inns Virginia is noted for, since I have an extra day off from work. Surely I deserve more pampering than one night at a roadside motel after ten days in the wilderness. John, though, is on a mission—getting back to his young vines is his only focus—and we drive straight through to North Georgia.

At the farm the next morning, I go out with John to tote buckets of water to the small vines. I am surprised at how healthy the new plants appear. I hadn't seen them for almost three weeks, and they had sprouted leaves galore. But John is concerned about the unusually dry spring. "I thought you told me grapes love dry," I say as we fill the back of the pick-up truck with water buckets. John thought we'd never need irrigation in Rabun County; its high rainfall had been the biggest worry for wine grape cultivation. The new plants, in a rare drought year, need some water early in the growing season. Loading the back of the truck with water buckets becomes part of my job description, to Coach's great delight.

"Except for the glamour of toting buckets, I'd trade this job for planting flowers," I say to John, who is far too intent on his vines to respond.

I leave early for my drive back to Atlanta. I might have stayed at the farm for the Sunday night cornbread and black-eyed peas supper that is ritual for John's dad—with a glass of buttermilk, of course—but I am ready for my city fix. I am annoyed that John doesn't sense that and travel to Atlanta with me for dinner and an overnight respite though I dare not suggest it. If he can't figure out this commute is a two-way street, I'm not going to tell him.

When I return to my condo, I pick up a pile of *New York Times*, put on some comfortable shoes and walk two miles up Peachtree Street to the only café I ever frequent alone, Intermezzo, mainly because I can occupy a small table in my favorite corner where I can read and not feel conspicuous. I order a plate of shrimp fettuccine and a glass of white wine and lose myself in the *Sunday Times* "Week in Review," catching up on national and international news before tackling the stack of Atlanta papers I'd picked up from my doorman when I returned. Later, I listen to a new recording of Aaron Copeland's "Appalachian Spring" and climb into bed from which a view of Atlanta's turreted city skyline welcomes me back to my high-rise Ansley Park apartment.

4

Married to the Earth

> Whither thou goest I will go; whither thou lodgest, I will lodge; your people will be my people. —*Ruth 1:16*

The next weeks and months fly past. John finds a young urologist in Rabun County with whom he can associate without forming any permanent partnership, pay a portion of the office overhead and work two or three days a week. The nearest hospital is a small one in Clayton, but John tells me there's a larger hospital in Toccoa, about a half hour away, where he can take more complex surgery, if necessary. I am encouraged that he feels a part-time country practice might work out—no question a financial squeeze awaits us if we are eventually to purchase the family farm from his siblings.

Toward the end of January, we head to Orange County, Virginia, for a long weekend to pick up more Norton cuttings. I am excited about finally meeting John's mentors, the Hortons. Some of the Virginia wineries we visit along the way make me feel as if I'm in the rolling hills of Tuscany or a forested rendition of Napa Valley. I have to admit they are pretty impressive. "Imagine the up-front capital these folks had to cough up," I say. "Are you thinking we can build a winery some day instead of just growing grapes?"

"Sure," John replies, as if I should have always known.

"We don't even have a plan for our new home on the farm yet," I respond in my *whatdayahmean* voice.

John doesn't say much, mumbling his standard, "We'll see." At least, I'd like to start the process of choosing a site for our new home on the farm, but getting the vineyard planted totally consumes John's thoughts.

We arrive at the Horton winery, an attractive stone structure, but John is so anxious to get out to the vineyards where Sharon Horton is pruning that I have little time to taste the Horton wines. An attractive, petite woman whose totally natural look tells me she loves being outdoors, Sharon welcomes John and me as if we'd all been friends for years. I am surprised that such a dainty woman can manage hundreds of acres of grapes—it's clearly no easy job. She hands John a pair of clippers and keeps on pruning vines as we talk. She patiently answers at least five or six questions he poses right away about how many shoots to leave on each cordon, the arm of the vine from which the new shoots grow, and she explains why she is leaving a spare shoot on the trunk of the vine below the wire—that shoot will grow into a cane that can become a substitute cordon in case one of the main cordons becomes weak or diseased. As she clips the long vertical canes that have borne this season's fruit down to stubby shoots hugging the old wood along the horizontal wire, some of the cut canes hang twisted and suspended on the wires above like an artist's wall hanging. "It saves time to come back through and pull those down later," she tells John, as she pauses to study the structure of the next vine before starting to cut.

Maybe it is the medical vibes—Sharon a former nurse, and John a physician—but she and John are clearly on the same wavelength. I feel like a fourth tire on a wheelbarrow, totally out of my milieu, but I can tell John loves the one-on-one lessons. Sharon exudes excitement over John's being such a quick study. "See, John," she says, "these *vinifera* are easy compared to the Norton. You just prune each cane to two buds—you only want eight or ten shoots on each arm." (She is referring to the old cordon that's hugging the horizontal trellis wire.) There are several workers on other rows, and John wants to know how long it takes to train them.

The wind comes up and I am freezing, but John and Sharon are oblivious to the elements as we walk clear across the vineyard to the Norton vines. They look totally different from the Cabernet Franc Sharon had been working on. The vines have a reddish hue and the canes lop downward over the Geneva Double Curtain trellis instead of growing upright as most of the *vinifera* do. The American vines are more tangled and—as Sharon describes them with a laugh—more disorganized. I note that her comment is similar to John's description of the Norton vines to the children and me over dinner last spring. It isn't getting any warmer, so I walk up and down a few more rows of vines, returning in time to hear Sharon explain that the Norton shoots coming off the old wood have to be cut alternatively to two buds and then five, still leaving no more than eight or nine of them to an arm.

"Why is that?" I ask, realizing I'd missed a key part of Sharon's lesson.

"Because the third and fourth bud on the Norton bear more fruit than the first and second," she explains, warning John also not to let any wine grape varieties "overcrop"—bearing too much fruit dilutes the intensity of the juice.

I wonder if any wine lovers we know care about such, but I can tell that John loves this stuff, a cocktail mix of winemaking science and basic farming.

Dennis is coming in from D.C. in the late afternoon, and the Hortons invite us to dinner at their favorite restaurant. Dennis brings a special bottle of wine to open with our meal, Horton Dionysus. It is wonderfully aromatic, rich and full bodied. I love the flowery nose, which Dennis attributes to the Portuguese Tinta Cao, a grape he only uses for blending and mostly with Touriga Nacional. Horton Dionysus, named for the god of wine, is only produced in an unusually good year, when the Touriga grapes, which he admits are tricky to grow, are near perfect. Dennis tells John he should try cultivating both Portuguese grapes—and John seems especially excited about the Touriga Nacional, the dominant grape in fine ports, from which Dennis makes an elegant dry red wine varietal.

"Some years, they'll rot before they get ripe enough," Dennis warns about the Touriga grapes. I can tell John counts that problem just another challenge.

Dennis and Sharon seem totally consumed with running their huge winery and vast vineyards. Dennis is clearly passionate about wine and about perfecting his grape growing. In addition to helping bring the Norton back to prominence, he is known nationally, I discover, as the "father of Viognier." He recommends Viognier to John as a white grape superior to the popular Chardonnay for our growing conditions in North Georgia. "Doesn't bud out as early in the spring and produces great fruit," he says, comparing it to his Chardonnay. That comment from an expert Southern wine grower makes me feel bad about hounding John to plant Chardonnay. I later learn from Sharon that Dennis is to be named one of the nation's forty top winemakers for his pioneering Viognier as a popular alternative to Chardonnay and a better bet for growers in the Southeast.

Dennis and John are fast friends by the end of our trip. I admire and enjoy Sharon, the savvy, soft-spoken vineyard manager. I had wondered how I'd feel about the Hortons, knowing Dennis is John's prime motivation for what still seems at times a crazy undertaking—cultivating fancy wine grapes in North Georgia. But I genuinely like the Hortons' warmth and authenticity. After meeting them, I understand where John has picked up his new passion for grape growing and wine making.

John and I fill the rusty farm truck bed with Norton cuttings and head back to Georgia on an icy Sunday. My main concern is to stay warm in the old truck whose unreliable heater has a mind of its own. When we stop at a Starbucks outside of Charlottesville, two dapper young men smirk as I hop out of the truck in my old parka, torn farm jeans and muddy boots. I am tempted to go over to their table to ask if they know where the outhouse is!

A week later, Joyce and Wayne come over again to help us with the second batch of Norton at the greenhouse. After tending the tiny plants, we hike together to John's and my favorite waterfall, Hemlock Falls at Moccasin Creek State Park, just a short distance from the farm. We return to the farmhouse for a hearty soup and homemade wheat bread as if we were true woods people. Joyce wonders out loud, however, how I am going to like "the country life." She and I have Atlanta Symphony season tickets together and sometimes snag our husbands to join us, taking in dinner before the concert. "What will you do without our favorite ethnic restaurants?" she asks. "Oinker's Barbecue," I reply gleefully, referring to the local hang-out down the highway.

John can hardly wait to see if what he learned from rooting the last batch of Norton cuttings will work. When spring comes, he is ecstatic. Almost 90 percent of the cuttings leaf out; we have 432 Norton plants to fill another six rows. I can't wait to help him plant them. I begin to spend more time in the vineyards with John, tying young plants to green plastic poles carefully spaced eight feet apart, pinching suckers off the trunks, the extra growth that sucks energy from the cordons that produce the buds of spring. The cordons that stretch along the horizontal wires need to grow strong in order to support the new canes that will bear grapes. John shows me how to work the "tapener," a gizmo like a large stapler that allows securing the vines with a flexible tape to the proper wire or post without breaking or squeezing them.

On this crisp spring morning in our vineyard, John and I are working on the Touriga Nacional, the Portuguese grape Dennis recommended to him. John opened a bottle of Touriga from the Portuguese Duro for my birthday dinner last fall, and I thought it was elegant.

I am determined now to get acquainted with our Touriga vines, and as I spend time working in them, I take note of the exquisite leaf which has a distinct and deeply indented lobe, five lobes with edges like rims of tiny rick-rack all around. We shake dirt and leaves from our shirts and head to the farmhouse for a lunch break, stopping to admire a patch of tiny purple hyacinths alongside the road. I ask John if he is thinking of planting a white grape, knowing he has rejected my earlier plea that he try some Chardonnay. "A number of Virginia wineries are producing Viognier, including Horton," he replies, "and I'm thinking about trying it."

I admit that I like the Virginia Viogniers I've tasted—Horton's and a couple of others. Some have lovely citrus and apricot flavors while still dry and crisp. "I think we first need to be sure we're doing okay with the red varieties we've already planted," John continues. "By the way, this afternoon, I want you to help me get some fertilizer out on the new vines."

"The glamour of owning a vineyard never ends, does it?" I reply with a laugh.

I know I am not going to be a winemaker, but when I have free time during the week in Atlanta, I am studying wine characteristics, reading and refining my tasting knowledge. I am certain I will better appreciate the uniqueness of each of our grape varieties if I spend more time with John in the vineyards.

One spring Sunday afternoon, after taking a short hike on the mountain to pick flame azalea, the most brilliant of orange blossoms in the world, I help pinch off more suckers on the trunks of the vines. "Didn't we just do this a couple of weeks ago?" I say to John. He nods and repeats Sharon's warning to leave two shoots on each trunk for spares in case something happens to the cordon on the wire above where the grapes will grow. As the grapes leaf out, I pay attention to the contrast in leaf shapes between the Cabernet Franc and the Malbec. The Cabernet Franc leaves have five lobes with distinctive "fingers," similar to the Touriga, while the Malbec leaves are larger with more subtle rounded lobes.

The next weekend I spend two whole days helping train the 246 Tannat plants. Grape vines know what their primary mission is—so even in their second "leaf " (second spring of budding out) they are making teeny green berry clusters. We have to pinch the clusters off because the young vines should not bear fruit, John says, until their third " leaf." Well, that's coming right up—and thank heavens. Patience is not my virtue, but it is what starting a vineyard requires. It breaks my heart to do it, but I dutifully throw the precious little clusters on the ground, wondering if this is symbolic of where our vineyard is headed financially. I ask John why the Tannat seem so much more prolific than its French sisters.

"Wait until you see the clusters mature," he replies. "Tannat produce huge clusters of grapes that are so tight, perfectly formed, and inky dark that you think they can't be real when you first come upon them. They have a whole different character from the other *vinifera*, more robust larger grapes with deep purple juice and thicker, redder stems." He explains that Tannat originates in southwest France, the Madiran region near the Pyrenees. That region, he says, has cold winters and is generally wetter than Bordeaux or Burgundy.

"Hey—maybe it's like Tiger," I reply, wishing for a Madiran of the South.

I decide the Tannat vines, with larger, deeper green leaves, are more masculine than not and I mutter to them to stop showing off, to stop putting out so many superfluous shoots and costing me so much time bending over and wrestling with every vine. When I move to the Cabernet Franc, I say only complimentary things and in my broken French. The vines grow upright, canes reaching for the sky in perfect symmetry. The leaves are evenly spaced.

"*Tu est elegant*," I say as I learn a different pattern of taping and caring for vines that seem so proper. The Malbec are much like the Cabernet Franc in their growth pattern, restrained and disciplined. Sharon has already warned John that the Malbec, which have thin skins, will ripen early and are more finicky than the Cabernet about weather and disease.

A couple of Atlantans who collect wines and attend the High Museum Wine Auction stop by the vineyard one day because they have heard John is growing Malbec. They are sure that is impossible to grow Malbec in Georgia. John explains that his Malbec, French clones, will never produce the robust, "chewy" Malbec wine that comes from Argentina where it is often spelled with a "k," "Malbeck." The French Malbec, he tells them, grow well in Virginia and are sometimes called "Cot" in France.[5] Malbec, John tells our visitors, makes an earthy, musty wine with lush berry aromas. It's a perfect fit, he declares, for our Blue Ridge Mountain *terroir* and our farm where berries of all kinds thrive.

I can tell how much John enjoys talking about the vineyards and the different varieties of grapes with people who love wine and have an interest in how to grow fine wine grapes in the South. The visitors are flabbergasted to see *vinifera* thriving in North Georgia.

As I work in the vineyards, I feel the soil and rocks between my fingers, smell the clover, pick the wild daisies that pop up randomly between the rows, and nurse dozens of scratches from thorny weeds. And I begin to think about the women who have worked this land before me. I develop a keener appreciation for John's mother, Ruth, and his grandmother, Tallulah, whom I classify as original farm-to-table advocates. They spent long hours in the kitchen not for lack of other interests—both were well educated and avid readers—but to make the most of the natural foods of each changing season, reward in itself.

My Southern Baptist upbringing comes home to me, and I recall the story about Ruth in the Bible who left her land of Moab to travel with her mother-in-law to Bethlehem in Judea, telling Naomi, *your people will be my people.* They arrived in Bethlehem in time for the barley harvest. Surely Ruth must have also said "your land shall be my land," though

---

[5] Jancis Robinson, *Oxford Companion to Wine* (New York: Oxford University Press, 1994) 593.

I can't really find such a statement by Ruth recorded in any version of the Bible. At any rate, the Arrendale-Ezzard farm becomes my land because it is John's land even though, Lord knows, I do not see my role as that of the dutiful and obedient wife of biblical description. My mother-in-law and John's grandmother peeled, chopped, preserved, and canned because they felt a kinship with the land and its bounty—squash, tomatoes, sweet corn, okra, berries, apples—all that it so reliably produced. I have spent a large part of my life as an outspoken feminist, rejecting what I deemed the old-fashioned apron image, but it finally occurs to me that my mother-in-law gave the same degree of perfection to farm food preparation as she did to completing her PhD dissertation. When she was alive, I wanted no part of her endless hours in the kitchen, although I enjoyed our discussions of her intellectual pursuit to attain a doctorate degree, after her five children were grown. Now that I'm learning farm ways, I wish I had paid attention to exactly how she made watermelon rind preserves, zucchini relish, corn pudding, and other delights—recipes stored in her head and not on recipe cards.

As I reach the end of the last row of Tannat, my back aches and I look up at the mountain in time to see wispy pink clouds forming behind it in the late afternoon sun. No wonder my back hurts and John's doesn't—he focuses only on the structure of the vines and could care less about the stubborn weeds I'm bending down to pull as I go. John says the vines are too young to risk putting out weed killer under them and that a few weeds aren't going to hurt anything. But I know the clover and daisies, so random and charming now, will lose the battle with weeds as the summer months ensue. I want our vineyards to be the most beautiful of agricultural endeavors ever.

John starts gathering the vineyard tools and clippers, and walks back to the farmhouse. We look back to admire the pattern of the rows of vines on the hillside beyond the barn. They resemble a colorful Appalachian quilt pieced together with perfectly spaced rows of vines reflecting patches of sunlight and shade. The mountain is just beginning to flaunt the first chartreuse swaths of budding trees, spring colors that will transform into a hundred shades of vibrant green before the end of May. Daffodils peep up near the old oak trees behind the creamery building as we head up the hill toward the weathered gray chicken shed behind the farmhouse where John keeps equipment.

"You know Poppa thinks this hill is the best place to view the whole farm," I say to John. "It could be a great picnic spot, but who would want to sit up here with all of this rusted farm equipment lying around? Why don't you get Coach to haul it off?"

"I will sometime," John replies. "That's not nearly as important as getting my vines cared for right now."

I sulk silently. It seems my dreams of the farm as I want to see it are always on hold.

I turn to the reality awaiting me as we enter the farmhouse back door. The sheets and towels I've brought from my apartment are in a heap on top of the dryer. (I've never bought a washer and dryer for my apartment and am forever hauling my laundry to the farm on weekends as if I were still a commuting college kid.) I scrounge up some leftover pot roast and potatoes for our dinner and turn to packing the car, a chore I hate. John folds the laundry for me while I start rinsing the dishes and loading the dishwasher. Suddenly, I feel something sharp as I reach for one last pot to wash. I look at my left hand only to see the four prongs of my wedding ring devoid of the diamond.

I let out a cry that brings John rushing to the sink beside me.

"Don't worry," he says with a big hug. "We'll find it." Tears begin to roll down my cheeks. It isn't as if it were the world's largest diamond, but it can't be replaced. John was a senior medical student when I left my promising media post at the NBC station in Atlanta, WSB television, to marry him the Christmas before he graduated.

"It just has to be in the Tannat vines," I whisper. "That's where I spent most of the afternoon." I can't face having to drive to Atlanta now; I'll just have to get up at 5:30 in the morning. I fall in bed with John still trying to comfort me. I think about the evening he gave me the ring, and I finally fall asleep snuggled up beside him knowing this farm-boy surgeon hasn't changed a bit and never will.

I leave the next morning before it is light, but hours and days and many phone calls later, John and I give up on finding the diamond. When John offers to replace it, I insist it is irreplaceable and declare that I'd rather spend the money on art for our new home-to-be in the vineyard. The following weekend I walk again up and down every row of Tannat, wondering if my diamond is happily nestled in an intricate root reaching deeper each day into the Tiger earth.

Somehow I like the shape of the Tannat leaves best of all—bolder and rounder, with uneven edges curling downward. Tannat, I am certain, is destined to be my favorite wine.

We keep looking, but my diamond never shows its sparkling head. For better or worse, I am now married to the earth at Tiger Mountain.

5

Smudge Pots and Brown Buds

Although he doesn't know it at the time, John is a pioneer in rooting Norton vines from cuttings. Many start-up Southern grape growers begin to contact him for advice about planting Norton. John enjoys advising those who come to our vineyards to pick up Norton cuttings in the winter; many of them send us pictures of their new vineyards with pathetic looking sticks in the ground waving a leaf or two beside forlorn poles. They are just as excited as we were about the first spindly growth.

Norton is a grape that will make you proud in just a couple of years with its deep green leafy canopy lush and full and its vigorous canes reaching out in all directions. In fact, it's too vigorous, and it takes a lot of shoot thinning to control it to harvest quality fruit.

It is during our Norton vineyard's second leaf when John discovers he can't get the tractor between some of the rows. The reason, although Coach is loath to admit it, is that the two of them had relied on Coach's alleged twelve-foot board to measure the distance between the rows when they were installing trellises. The problem was that Coach had *two* boards in the back of his pick-up—a twelve-foot board and a ten-foot board—and had pulled out the wrong one for spacing some of the rows. John finds it impossible to drive his tractor or sprayer between six of the Norton rows, which are only ten feet apart.

Once he discovers the error, John is despondent, a rare state for him. Not even his favorite mashed potatoes and chicken gravy I make for a "comfort food" dinner cheer him. We have planted 792 Norton vines, and he is already putting in long days, with help only from Coach since I'm in Atlanta all week. (It would be another eight years before we pull up 194 Norton plants to widen the rows so we can get the tractor through to spray and tend the vines properly.)

It's early April—the canes on the vines are "bleeding" as the tiny buds wake to another spring and begin to swell. To walk through the rows is to absorb the energy and anticipation that something is about to happen. There is nothing routine about bud break; it's always fresh and challenging—as if a new movement of a great musical composition is being created each spring.

"I've got to get back to Denver next week," John tells me, "and I sure hate to leave at bud break." Then he shares more bad news. The young urologist our son-in-law has recruited to replace John in the practice has decided to go into academic medicine.

"The practice is too much for one guy, and I can't leave Brian stranded," he says. "Finding the right partner isn't easy." I get the significance of what John is saying: our two-year commute is turning into a three-year commute. I try to focus on the immediate problem.

"Don't worry," I reply. "I'll be here at the farm the next two weekends. Coach and I can take care of the vineyards. If necessary, I'll find a way to come up during the week."

Many of our buds are already showing that fragile pink color that marks the beginning of a new vintage. The weather forecast for the weekend after John leaves gives a chance of frost. In Atlanta, I go back to the office Thursday evening and work on a Sunday editorial until midnight so I can get away early Friday. The temperature drops to 34 degrees Friday evening and is supposed to be about the same Saturday evening. But for Sunday, the forecast is for a low of 22 degrees. Coach and I spend most of Saturday collecting huge metal containers from friends and various hardware stores in the county since we don't have any bona fide smudge pots. The difference, of course, is that these metal containers will mostly put heat out the top and not much out the sides. We place twenty-four of them in differing shapes, sizes, and colors around the vineyards. Unfortunately, I have an 8:00 interview with a U.S. senator Monday morning that I don't feel I can cancel or dump on an editorial colleague, so I have little choice but to leave Sunday evening. Coach hires a neighboring farm worker who agrees to stay up all night and man the smudge pots (since that's not something Coach, now in his seventies, is about to do).

Sure enough, the dreaded freeze forecast comes true. Our friend stokes the fires most of the night—to little avail. I spend a restless night in Atlanta, hardly sleeping a wink. Coach arrives at the farm around 6:30 the next morning and calls me about 7:00. He reports the worst: "They look dead as a doorknob," he says, describing our delicate pink buds as brown and drooping. John assures us from Denver that all is not lost.

"Grapes have a second bud," he says. "It's not like they are Grandpa's apple trees, gone for the season." We both know we have yet another year before we can harvest our grapes anyhow, but we also know if the vines were more mature, a freeze like this one would greatly diminish our yield, second buds or not.

The next weekend, Coach and I commiserate over the brown buds, but John has instructed Coach to pinch them off. Thankfully, not all of the Norton or the Malbec are budded out and in the late ripening Mourvedre, buds are just beginning to swell. Coach can't resist pointing out to me, though, that the Concord eating grapes on the hill by the woods—"above the frost line," whatever that means—are too smart to have budded out so early in April, despite the warm March.

John is back by the end of the month and isn't as alarmed about the state of our vineyard as I am. A year from this coming fall, though, we'll undertake our first harvest. Still, he and other farmers in the area say such a devastating freeze in April is rare.

Sure enough, some of the nipped shoots begin to show a late fuzzy bloom in early May. (Grape blooms are always fuzzy, reminding me of dandelions.) As the teeny grape clusters develop, that wispy bloom is essential for "berry set," the filling out and maturing of the clusters. But John admits the second bud "confuses" the vine, producing grapes that ripen later than those from a primary bud.

It's year two of our grand venture, and so much is on hold. We are still planting more grapes, and we must wait three falls to pick the first ones. We must wait for our Denver son-in-law to find the right doctor to replace John before he can move back to the farm full time; we must wait until we sell our Denver home before we start to build a new home on the farm. After two and a half years of commuting, I can hardly wait for both of us to be back in Georgia even if it means living out of boxes between the farmhouse and my Atlanta apartment.

My daughter Lisa, always the philosopher, tells me I should enjoy the process, the doing, the becoming of the vineyard; she knows I like contracts and deadlines and am too goal oriented, often forgetting to pause and enjoy the "now."

Just when I'm feeling every day is a holding pattern with our grape growing venture at the farm, I undertake a new writing project at the newspaper outside the scope of my normal editorial and column writing. Thanks to Ron Martin, the editor of the *Journal-Constitution*, there is an open opportunity for any writer to submit an idea for an in-depth series of articles and to get adequate time to research it, think about it, and write it—surely an anomaly in the fast-moving daily news world. One of the things I admire most about Martin is his unwavering commitment to fine writing. He is not, as are so many editors, obsessed with the political topic *du jour.*

On a lark, I submit an idea to write about trees, to collect Southern tree stories, thinking it's surely too ho-hum to be accepted. But having written dozens of editorials about the sad loss of native hardwoods in the city to Atlanta's never-ending suburban development and ever-expanding shopping malls, and having tediously opined in daily editorials for stronger county-by-county tree ordinances to ameliorate urban "hot spots," storm water runoff and what looks like the paving over of "the city of trees," I decide Southerners' attachment to trees is more emotional than scientific or political. Every Southerner has a tree story, and I think stories rather than studies and ordinances are the best way to raise public awareness of the value of trees.

In the old days, my South Georgia grandfather gave directions by way of trees—turn right at the red oak and left at the old magnolia. John's grandfather, the county surveyor, made surveying maps with lines from a maple tree to a sweet gum stump. Once my project is accepted by a group of editors, I find stories of individuals and communities who have gone to extraordinary lengths to raise money or stage protests to save just one tree. The research and the people I talk to take me to a new level of understanding the human connection to all growing things, even grape vines—a love of land and of all plant life that is a good deal more complex than just shade and beauty or berries and fruit.

My project editor, Thomas Oliver, likes the idea I suggest of sleeping in the top of a tree to kick off my tree series—not by myself, of course, but with five members of Tree Climbers International, who can train me in how to use ropes to climb up and can secure the heavy hammocks for an overnight in branches that are safe to hold them. I like Oliver's idea to call my series "The Trees of Our Lives."[6]

"It's the kind of writing you love," says John, "colorful characters and lot of outdoors. Maybe you'll spend the night just a branch away from a woodpecker—you should be conditioned for that from my snoring." He seems not the least bit worried about my overnight seventy-five feet high in a hundred-year-old tulip poplar.

I start by interviewing a University of Georgia professor and noted author, Kim Coder, at the School of Forestry. During an interview, Coder tells me we have to learn a lot about ourselves to understand trees because "through our tenure on earth, we've given this ancient plant form a soul" *Wow*, I think to myself as he talks and shares some of his writing, *maybe grape vines have a spiritual dimension too.* I know my husband has a near sacred feeling about the farm, the dirt and rocks and weeds themselves. But I'm certain it's the wine grower who adds soul to the grapes and the wines they produce.

As our vineyard slowly recovers from the spring freeze, and as our hectic commute from Denver to Atlanta wears on into its third year, I'm able to lose myself again in my writing—finding among other extraordinary trees, the state's oldest black oak, a tree General Sherman missed when he burned Atlanta. It now shades the patio of a Catholic hospice located in the central city in the shadow of Turner Field.

"People go to 'Our Lady's Oak' to die," I write after

---

[6] Martha Ezzard, "The Trees of Our Lives," (Seven-Part Series) *Atlanta Journal-Constitution*, Oct. 31–Nov 7, 1999.

visiting the hospice and talking with some of the staff and patients. I gather stories about the daily strength and comfort the tree offers the dying.

I find a blue-collar community fighting to save old trees set to be destroyed by a school district that wants to clear-cut part of Connolly Park in the College Park area of Atlanta to build a school. Some in the community take a day off work without pay to show up at an administrative hearing to fight for conservation of the giant hardwood trees in their neighborhood park; the trees, they argue, belong to the public, not one government entity. I ride MARTA, the underground, with them to the hearing. They win their battle, and the tree climbers group places a time capsule in the top of a three-hundred-year-old oak tree in the park with my name on it—their way of thanking me for the editorials I wrote championing their cause. In another part of the city, despite vigils and protests, Decatur citizens lose the battle to save a two-hundred-year-old oak, which is cut down at night—lest protesters sit in it—by shopping center developers in their hurry to make way for a Walmart.

The last story I write teaches me even more about the human passion for planting and growing things. I visit with Tom Cox, a suburbanite who has created a multicultural arboretum of six hundred trees from thirty-eight countries. When he starts talking about his *Heptacodium Miconioides,* the seven-son tree of Korea, I'm know I'm entering a new world. He touches its starry white blossom lightly and strokes its smooth bark, pointing to the subtle streaks of orange in its trunk. The tree, he tells me, is a Korean symbol of peace. A man in his mid-fifties, Cox's excitement about his arboretum creation is akin to John's excitement about his vineyard creation—both are boys on grand adventures who are awed and inspired as they nourish and tend. My favorite tree at the arboretum is the paper bark maple with thin bark that peels in scroll-like fashion until ringlets fall all around its reddish trunk and limbs. I resolve to plant one at the farm, and I have the perfect spot for it—just outside my study window.

"Wait 'til you see this one," Cox says to me for about the tenth time as he scampers from tree to tree.

"What does this arboretum mean to you personally?" I ask, knowing that garden clubs from all over schedule tours and events there.

"This is my legacy," he says. "Some people leave music, some leave books—I leave trees."[7] His joy is in the doing of it, not necessarily any goal, as I tell John later when we're into another "where are we going with this vineyard?" telephone conversation.

John and I had promised not to let more than two weeks go by without seeing each other during our commute, an agreement we didn't always keep given our separate career demands. When I fly to Denver several weeks after that scary April vineyard frost and while I'm still in the middle of my tree project, John meets me at the airport and whisks me to our favorite French restaurant.

Funny, I think, *he didn't do that when I was just hanging out in Denver.*

---

[7] Ibid., Nov. 7, M-1.

6

A Crow in the Freezer

In early May, I vow to try scaring off the swallows that return in increasing numbers each year to build their nests in our barn. Birds I generally love, but the mess the barn swallows make is an ongoing challenge. The swallows are in a totally different category from the feathered friends whose songs I learned when backpacking on the Appalachian Trail. They are, to my way of thinking, nuisance birds, an ever-growing tribe descending on the barn *en masse* every spring, building their mud and straw nests in the rafters and leaving a mighty mess below. I have a hard time convincing Coach of this good-bird, bad-bird distinction. Baby swallows chirping from mud nests, a stray cat, a rooster when he can find one, and his horse, Crown—all together in the old Ezzard barn—are perfect bliss for him. Never mind the piles of manure, the dirty straw on the floor, the caked-on remnants of a hundred bird visits, and the piles of wood and nails from a dismantled chicken shed he meant to repair years ago.

Though John and I have already contracted to have the old barn—built by his father and grandfather just after World War II—repaired and painted, the interior is in sad condition. That matters not to Coach; all he cares about is the return of the barn swallows to tell him spring has arrived.

"Don't you know these little birds come all the way from Chile and choose our barn to raise their young'uns?" he scolds when I start to knock down some of last year's nests, hoping to at least thin the population of new birds. When I bring in some large plastic owls that a local Reeves Hardware clerk advises me will "scare the bejesus" out of barn birds, Coach just shakes his head.

"I don't want anything bad to happen to the swallows, Coach, but we'd enjoy fewer of them more," I say, feeling a little mean about my anti-swallow tactics.

Coach holds the wires dutifully and silently while I climb up on a ladder to hang the owls near the front and back entry gates to the barn.

"Well, here's the good news," I say, refraining from any mention of cleaning the inside of the barn, which I hope he will help with when the outside repairs are done. "John didn't like my choice of gray paint any better than you did; so we're going to go with barn red for the exterior."

In fact, when I had arrived the prior Friday afternoon, John greeted me motioning glumly as I got out of my car to follow him to the barn. "You want to see the battleship *Missouri*?" he asked. I had to admit the side of the barn towards the farmhouse that had a new coat of steel gray paint reminded me of a mausoleum. John had argued for red from the beginning, but I thought gray would blend in with the environment and I didn't want our historic barn to look like the red pre-fab ones that dot the county. I admit that John is right; the gray looks absolutely mournful, so I readily agree to go with his choice of red. The trim will be white and the roof metal. Would that our house plans could be so speedily decided upon.

At one point, I had discussed making the barn our new home, with metal revolving doors in the old silo and bedrooms on the first floor in horse stall layout. We could keep the wide, middle corridor, which could lead to three-story glass windows and doors and a deck looking out on Tiger Mountain. The living quarters and kitchen could be upstairs in order to make the most of the cathedral-like wood-beamed hayloft. John never seriously considered my notion. "Even Peter Mondavi couldn't pay the heating bill," he had commented when I showed him my photo of a silo entry to a gorgeous New England farmhouse a friend had brought me from an architectural magazine.

"Worse yet," John had said with a chuckle, "imagine telling Coach that Crown is going to be homeless."

Whenever we talk of a home site that would face the pristine Tiger Mountain, there is always the nagging worry about what encroaching development may do to our now-precious vista. We own a little piece of Tiger Mountain, but not enough, we fear, to save it from the plethora of homes and cabins hanging off the sides of so many of North Georgia's defaced mountains, roads being cut through ridge lines and the rest. I'd written a dozen editorials about the need for mountain protection laws in Georgia, to little avail in a state where "local control" and "property rights" are the political mantra. A mountain protection law was passed during the tenure of former governor Zell Miller, but it required local implementation that didn't happen in our county. Later, even the watered-down law was repealed.

Coach reluctantly puts the ladder away for me after the owls are hung, sensing he may have the last laugh if they don't work. He knows by now that I have made it my mission to beautify the farm, and there's no hiding that he's not happy about any farm maintenance that requires him to get off of his tractor or mower.

As we close the barn gate, Coach stops beside the new daylilies I've just put in at the corner of the barn and looks also at the two new cherry trees just beyond. "Hard to mow around those," he says, sweeping his arm in an exaggerated arc as if I'd planted hundreds of lilies and trees instead of half a dozen lilies and two measly trees. I go on about the bright color lilies I've chosen because I know he could easily mow them down "accidentally."

Just as I'm dusting the dirt, hay, and feathers off my jeans, two nicely dressed women drive up in an old Lincoln. They are from the Methodist Women's Auxiliary, and they've come by to say welcome to "Dr. Ezzard's wife."

"I'm Martha," I say, extending my hand to one. They both seem a little taken aback about a handshake, but it only takes me a minute to remind myself that Southern women hug or put their arms on your shoulders. Handshakes are still male business protocol to them. The handshake thing is almost automatic for me in my careers at the law firm and the newspaper, but after all, stepping out of the barn in my torn jeans is hardly like stepping out of my office. I quickly ask them to join me for a cup of tea at the farmhouse. After some brief conversation, I tell them how much the family appreciates all that the Clayton Methodist Church did for John's mom in her last days and assure them that John and I will continue to accompany Poppa to the Sunday worship services when we can. I gently decline their invitation to join the Women's Auxiliary, explaining that I still work full time in Atlanta during the week.

Later I tell Coach the visit from the church women has convinced me it's time to clean the horse stall in the barn where he is prone to camouflage old manure by piling new hay on top.

I might as well be asking favors of the cement silo.

"Now, Maah-tha," he drawls with that mischievous glint in his eyes that makes it impossible for me to be mad with him, "don't you fret about these little things so, you know I'm gonna will you my half of the farm."

On the heels of that good ol' boy conversation comes a similar episode a few days later involving crows in the sweet corn. Although John and I have planted grape vines on the rolling hills where acres of Silver Queen corn recently stood, about a half acre of corn remains at the far end of the newly planted vines.

John has hired Winfred McKay, a talented local builder to redo the barn. He was recommended to us by my *Atlanta Journal-Constitution* editor and his wife, whose second home—a contemporary masterpiece of earth tones, glass, and light—McKay had built just thirty minutes north of us. Though we have no architect for our new home yet, we know McKay worked with some top-notch Harvard architects on that house, and we have our eye on him for building our home as well. McKay mentions a wood craftsman, Peter Bull, who lives in nearby Cleveland, Georgia. McKay thinks we should talk to Peter when we start planning a kitchen. He also recommends a metal craftsman, Frank Darnell, who did a lot of work on my editor's home that McKay built. I know the Darnell tractor repair shop and ask him if he's the same man who built the wondrous fireplace of stainless steel that we've admired on the large screened-in porch at the Martin home. Darnell, it turns out later, is also able to build us a corkscrew leg of stainless steel on the bar in our winery tasting room from a simple drawing we give him. John has known the Darnell family in Rabun County for a long time, and he counts on Frank and his son, Dexter, to repair his tractor. But like many artisans in the mountains, their true creative talents are little known. One day when Frank comes over to talk to John, he takes particular note of a large copper wire basket I bought at a crafts show in Atlanta. When John tells him I plan to hang it on the wall as an art piece, he scratches his head and says with a chuckle, "Well, John, I reckon I've been throwin' all my art away."

Though they are enormously talented, there is nothing pretentious about the Darnells or about McKay, who knows the best of the local craftsmen, whether stone masons or cabinetmakers. After all, this is the Appalachians where there is a long tradition of knowing how to create with your hands—from weavings, afghans, quilts, and sweaters to furniture and structures of native hardwoods, rock, and stone. The mountain artisans I soon find to be masters of combining precision with art. I vow to use as many of them as we can when we build our home. (John and his siblings are no exceptions to the use-your-hands tradition. I remember the chief of urology saying when John finished his residency that John had "the finest surgical hands" of anyone he had trained recently.)

One reason John and McKay hit it off so well is that McKay loves fishing, hunting, and growing sweet corn as well as anything in the world. When John complains that the crows are eating our sweet corn and that our scarecrow seems worthless so far, McKay advises him to shoot a couple of crows and hang a dead one in the corn field.

"I'll tell you what, John," he says, "I always keep a dead crow in the freezer this time of year." I put my hand over my mouth to keep from gasping. *A dead crow in the freezer?* I imagine running into one tucked between the ice cream and the orange juice.

John is an avid fisherman but not a hunter and doesn't even own a gun. He gets his brother, Henry, to bring him a dead crow, and he follows McKay's advice. I can hardly stand looking at the disgusting thing amidst our corn stalks, but it actually works. The crows disappear, and our sweet corn is bountiful. But I am quick to nix any spare crows in the freezer.

7

A Cardboard House with Two Towers

A nice offer on our Denver home comes sooner than we had expected and causes John to get serious about building our "dream" home in the vineyards at Tiger. I am pleasantly surprised when he announces that he and our son-in-law have worked out a schedule that will enable him to spend every other month at the farm and that he will be moving to Tiger full-time within six months. I pull out my worn magazine clippings of house ideas when John agrees we should look for an architect. I had already talked with Atlanta friends about two architects whose work I admire.

I approach the house building with some trepidation, however. The bitterest arguments John and I ever had were over the purchase of the three homes we lived in since we married. While I worry now about our spending on the vineyards, John has always been the penny-pincher about spending on houses, clothes, and cars. He still reminds me that I declared, "I hate this house," as we were moving into our first home when he started his practice in Denver. He had refused to consider a slightly more expensive and a thousand times more charming house in a well-established neighborhood. The one we bought instead was a tract house in a near treeless suburban development where I could see my neighbor's hamburger grill from our patio. Within a year after we moved in, I found a home in Cherry Hills Village, the community where we raised our family over the next twenty years. It was a traditional two-story home on a dirt road cul-de-sac that backed up to woods and a creek—and was still only ten minutes from John's medical office. When I first showed John the house, set among mature trees but located at the bottom of a hill, he said, "Who would want to live in that damn hole?" He relented only because the Cherry Creek public school system was, and still is, one of the best in the country and our oldest daughter, Shelly, was ready for first grade. The house was a bit of a financial stretch and we did without furniture in the living room, except for our cherished piano, for almost two years. I was pregnant with our third child when we moved in, and while the comfortable traditional house with two fireplaces on Cherry Vale Drive was never my dream home, it was the ideal neighborhood for raising a young family. We subsequently leased eight acres in the flood plain by the creek behind us, and built a barn so our girls and some neighborhood children could have horses and enjoy the local pony club.

Almost two decades later, we moved to a hundred-year-old house in downtown Denver's Capitol Hill, a wonderfully diverse and colorful neighborhood where I could ride my bike to my Larimer Square law office, but John had a longer drive to his Cherry Hills office. The main reason he didn't complain about the radical move from a quiet suburban area to the inner city one was because we were able to sell the Cherry Hills home for more than we paid for the city home—though I have to give him credit for always being open to change, an attitude we share. Our Ninth Avenue home was our "adult" sophisticated house, one a talented decorator had remodeled for herself. Its huge rooms and high ceilings, complete with Victorian "tooth" molding, were set off with bright, oversized silk window coverings, more contemporary than not, bleached oak floors, a copper bar and stunning kitchen with marble floor. It was located on the edge of Capitol Hill's historic district, a mixed neighborhood of historic homes filled with interesting professional people and a smattering of ugly apartment buildings. It was also only two blocks from a seedy grocery store.

Despite our house battles past, I am encouraged that John is bent on making a dramatic statement with our home-to-be. "It has to speak to the vineyards," he says.

We invite one particular architect couple to come to the farm for a picnic. We walk the farm property and talk about the kind of house and the site that would reflect our relationship with the land, the vibrant colors and shapes of trees on the mountain, the earthy richness of moss and leaves and loamy black soil, the irregular ripples of the mountain ridges in storm and sun, the ancient bruised rocks at the base of the mountain that anchor and comfort us. Two key things we take from these talented architects—that the core of daily living is how the light falls in different seasons and at different times of day on a home and what vistas, from lush green vines in summer to stark twisted gray canes and hayfields in winter, we want to frame from the inside out. And the barn, oh, the magnificent barn, such a huge part of our landscape; restoring it should be our first investment, these architects tell us.

When they leave, I discover the barn advice is about all John and I can agree upon. "But they are masters of light and of the contours of the land," I plead.

John simply nods and says, "Yeah, but our budget just may not be on their radar." He did find them as interesting and creative as I did—so we let that conversation be for the moment.

The second architect I invite to the farm also gives us excellent advice. We had considered remodeling the rock farmhouse, thinking we could build a house around a house, making the dappled brown and gray outside rock that came from Tiger Mountain the inside walls in some innovative way and adding a huge expanse of glass on the back facing the still pristine view of the mountain. Poppa is all for our remodeling the farmhouse, but now and then, he'd say, "Do whatever you want, but maybe leave the kitchen like it is." The small, cozy kitchen after all *is* his wife Ruth, whose bustle and laughter, chopping and peeling, steaming and frying made it the constant aromatic delight. I decide there is no way I can remodel the farmhouse while Poppa is still able to enjoy it.

This second architect confirms that right decision. He warns against trying to make the rock farmhouse something it isn't. It has charming proportions, he says, and they ought not be distorted. Organic and minimalist, speaking to the surrounding environment is this architect's milieu. He even goes so far as to suggest, after driving past the junk car lot by the post office (a Tiger eyesore), that we ought to incorporate not just native hardwoods, but plenty of metal in our new home! He wants us to express our closeness to the land by building a tri-level structure nestled into a hillside overlooking the pond where he is thrilled to spot egret and a red-winged blackbird.

As he drives away, John says, "He's talented and connected to the environment, all right, but he has a vision of the house *he'd* like to build, not the house *we* want to build."

"Well, we didn't really give him many specific ideas," I respond. "I want our home to reflect the feel of the earth, the shapes of the trees and rocks and the wonder of the wildlife around us, don't you?" I respond. I am already discouraged at John's lack of enthusiasm for retaining either of my selected architects. I moan to our artist daughter Shelly over the phone that I can't seem to get her father moving on the house design.

"Let me give it a try, Mom," she replies. "Maybe I can motivate him."

A few days later, just before he sets out for Denver again, John comes running in the house waving a magazine picture of a New Zealand vineyard at me. In the middle of lush green vines on rolling hills rises a sparkling contemporary home of light colored stucco with a soaring tower and unusual roof line. "This is it," he says. "I want a house with a tower in the vineyard."

Before I know it, John and Shelly have collaborated on a drawing that is truly unusual—a house with two clerestory towers and a roof line that in the abstract mimics the shape of Tiger Mountain and the ridges that ripple down from it.

When I arrive for a Denver weekend, John declares that Shelly should be our architect. I don't know what to say. The drawing is spectacular and I love it, but Shelly is an artist, not an architect. How can this possibly work?

"When I get back," John says when Shelly isn't around, "I'm going to talk with Winfred McKay about how we could pull this together, perhaps with a structural engineer to help Shelly."

To my surprise, Shelly tells me later that her father had actually figured out the precise angles of the unusual floor plan when she suggested a kitchen, family room, dining room, and living room all coming off a single point, with a three-way fireplace in the middle.

When we return to Tiger, John and I take some long walks on the farm looking at potential sites. I want to build a lot higher on the mountain than he does, so we can see the pond, but he says, "I want to be able to reach out and touch my vines." I decide he is right. And we choose a knoll just above the first two vineyards we've planted.

Since John is back and forth to Denver every other month, he and Shelly pore over house plans. I am once again totally absorbed in my writing; my column is now being distributed nationally by the *New York Times* news service, and I am immersed in research for another special editorial series. This one on indigent defense—Georgia's lack of a constitutional system to assure poor people accused of crimes have lawyers to defend them—a chance to put my legal skills to good use. In fact, I take no credit for the vision Shelly and John develop of the high ceiling angles, the three-way fireplace of glass to pull together the living room, dining room and family-kitchen area. There are to be two clerestory towers, one a library above the entry to the house and the other, slightly lower, over the dining room. Moonrises, sunrises and light will be glorious from the living room, dining room, and our bedroom—all of which face northeast. My sense of spatial dimension is so poor that I have a hard time visualizing the angles of the high ceilings and the size of the rooms from blueprints—though the living room size is copied from the Denver home I loved as is the staircase with its unique landing, just right for a sculpture we own.

Shelly comes to Tiger and confers with McKay. He treats her as if she were the most important architect in the world, and they often talk by phone. Meanwhile, John moves to the Tiger farmhouse full-time and starts his part-time country practice.

A stressful, sometimes hysterical, time of planning and building begins. I am living in Atlanta during the week and John is living in Tiger. He frequently calls me (when I'm writing on deadline) to demand an instant decision on some change in the house plan. How McKay and our daughter weather our disagreements is a mystery. I argue for some unique metal front doors and John wants wood with beveled glass panels. I want a two-story narrow window behind the staircase, which I declare should be open, but John nixes it as too pricey to build. Though John and I yell at each other over minute details, the house slowly and magically rises. Soon I can see that the profile of the roof from afar reflects, just as Shelly envisioned, the shape of Tiger Mountain.

The frame of the house rises on the knoll above the vineyards looking majestic even in skeleton form. I walk through it with John and Winfred and fret that the rooms are not as large as those in our Denver home. Measurements tell me I am dead wrong. At Christmas, Shelly presents me with a grand surprise—a perfect cardboard model of the house—like a dollhouse, with doors and windows that open to angular ceilings and the triangular fireplace. It is built to scale and I don't even want to think of the tedious hours Shelly put into it—while raising her young family and putting aside her own art.

When we get to the details of the kitchen, it's my time to work with Shelly. She finds a book, *The Art of Kitchen Design*,[8] the history of English kitchens; they are "furniture kitchens," places for families to live as well as cook and eat. I see Queen Anne legs on a stunning mahogany table to hold a stovetop that stretches out as a long counter from a round top at one end. I see an armoire for a refrigerator. Shelly explains that she wants to design this kind of kitchen as a contemporary version of the English style and we retain wood craftsman Peter Bull to work with her. My first priority is to be able to view the vineyards and barn from my kitchen stove.

On a cold New Year's Eve, John and I walk from the farmhouse up the moonlit hill to our unfinished house with a bottle of wine and our warm dinner in an insulated picnic bag. Amidst the wood shavings on the floor beside Darnell's metal skeleton of our unusual fireplace, we open a card table and light two candles, which John had sneaked up to the house earlier. "Now we're one with the land," I whisper.

---

[8] Johnny Grey, *The Art of Kitchen Design* (London: Oxford University Press, 1994).

"And never moving to any other place on earth," he replies. "Promise."

After thirty-five years of marriage, I can honestly say it is the most memorable New Year's Eve we ever spent together.

8

Poppa and Elvis: The End of an Era

The letter to the editor in the *Clayton Tribune* paid homage to an unknown farmer in Tiger. The writer said she was part of a relative's funeral procession, which wound its way down the two-lane Highway 441 and past rolling fields of corn and hay. As the procession approached, a farmer got down from his tractor and stood with his hat over his heart until all of the cars passed.

The farmer in the field was Poppa, of course. It was not a one-time gesture; it was his habit to halt his work when a funeral procession passed, whether the dead be stranger or friend. Born of his war years, his expression of honor for the dead was indicative of his deep respect for life.

All of the family had seen Poppa stop his farm work for funeral processions over the years. This vignette of him out in the fields, hat and hand over his heart, is only one of those that comes to mind on the late August day Poppa dies.

Poppa loved summer's end, and with fall's approach it was as if every cornstalk, their fruitful ears long gone and their season's work done, is bowing in the field to honor him. With vegetable and berry harvest over he should be sitting in his rocking chair on the front porch watching the morning mist rise from the creek, admiring his beloved blueberry bushes in the field across the road, their tiny leaves shimmering in the sunlight against golden mown hay. Fall's beginning is the culmination of farm work, apples growing plump, grapes hanging purple, late summer tomatoes still fat and saucy, clinging to life beside tall stalks of spent okra whistling in the wind. Gardens on the farm, except for bright orange pumpkins peeking out, are ready to be "lain by," plowed under until next year. It's the time Poppa could usually say goodbye to ten-hour tractor days, backbreaking weed pulling and hoeing around vegetables. It's the time when he could rock on the farmhouse porch and savor it all. It's the season for collecting sunflower and zinnia seeds for the spring to come. It's the beginning of a new growing cycle.

But Poppa's rocking chair stands empty this day—Tippy won't eat, and the deserted tractor in the field, despite the big round hay bales that surround it, looks forlorn.

"Poppa would have wanted us to celebrate the approach of autumn, with or without him," I say to my grieving husband, "because he understood so well that nature dies beautifully only to live again."

Poppa's recognition of the fragility of life and of its seasons was the result of his fighting three wars: World War II, Korea, and Vietnam. "The Colonel was about as in sync with the seasons of life on earth as a body can get," Coach says, shaking his head sadly as he joins our conversation on the farmhouse porch. He tries to console Tippy, who doesn't want to sit still but continues to roam aimlessly from porch to house to yard, looking for his beloved Colonel. Content to nourish the land, serve his country and his God, educate his family, his was the non-materialistic life, sometimes to the extreme. He once sent part of his cost-of-living military pension back to the federal government because it resulted in his making more money per month than the average active duty soldier. He was furious about such inequity.

"Like father, like son," I say to John and often not in his best moments. That is because the Colonel's value set, admirable as it was, didn't always include sensitivity to the small things that touch others. He focused on taking care of the big things, like college tuition for some poor kid who wouldn't otherwise get a shot at a college education, an interest-free loan, not a gift, mind you, to one of his children struggling with a young family. Would he buy a new car or a new set of dishes to make Ruth happy? Of course not—sheer luxury, not necessary. Would he help fund tuition for her to pursue a doctorate degree after raising five children? You bet. Poppa never had a credit card, never owned a share of stock. It was his lifelong habit to drop off his utility payments to the power company office when going to town—because it saved postage. But travel the world and love the people of other countries he did—people, yes, things, no. I find it easy to romanticize Poppa—to put aside some of his harshness and admire his adherence to loyalty, moral dignity, family, his respect for the earth, and all things that grow.

John is grieving that he didn't sense that Poppa wanted to die at home. Two days before his death, John brought him from his assisted living home, Traces of Tiger, to the farmhouse to see Tippy and rock in his favorite chair on the porch. He was wearing the streaked and faded once-red parka we gave him for Christmas more than twenty years ago. Of course, he had newer jackets family members had given him, but he always said when he left the others hanging in the closet and chose the tattered one instead, "It's still good, isn't it?" John helped him to the living room sofa where he lay down to nap. John thought he should get him back to his nighttime nursing care, where the family had nurses with him around the clock. He could neither walk alone nor speak clearly.

"He came home to die," John says now, "and I didn't get it."

Trying to console, I reminded John how proud Poppa was that his oldest son had come back to keep the family farm cultivated, to grow something. While Poppa never had a drink in his life, *growing something* was all that counted—wine grapes weren't an issue. (As John once told a reporter writing a story about the vineyard, "Poppa wouldn't have cared if I were growing marijuana. He was just happy I came back home to tend the farm.")

In this week of grief, our daughter Lisa begins to read some old letters in one of the boxes of Poppa's papers that we are going through. They are letters to her father when Poppa was in North Africa at the beginning of World War II. My husband was not even school age in July 1943, but Poppa was clear that he was the oldest son.

> Dear John,
>
> Your daddy is having a good time living in a tent with three other fellows. It has been mighty cold here though. How is your garden doing? Are you feeding "Porky" regularly? It won't be long before you can be in 4-H and

> enter Porky in competition. You will have to take Daddy's place around the farm for a while, old fellow, so you want to learn managing things. Remember that your daddy always thinks of you, though I can't write you very often. Be a good boy and say your prayers every night.
>
> Love,
> Daddy

Lisa, our writer and poet daughter, digs through more wartime letters—the ones that say "Sorry I can't make it home for your birthday" or "for Christmas." Some of the letters are from Poppa in Korea, and there is a particularly poignant one at Christmas with a black and white photograph of children singing "Silent Night" to Poppa and two other American soldiers.

Lisa also pulls from the blueberry box slivers of paper saved more recently. Some are IOUs and others a "hello to the Colonel." One is anonymous: "I have 2 favorite places in Georgia: sunset on Cumberland Isl. & berries @ your farm. Thank you!" The one we all love most is a longer note scrawled on a piece of lined paper torn from a small spiral notebook:

> I've been picking from your field for over 20 years & thought it was time I said "thank-you" for being such good stewards of the piece of Eden the Lord has given you & for blessing families like mine in the process—especially at a price large families can afford. I hope you are well blessed for your hard work. Thanks!

Jan Tu, now Jane Chang, visits shortly after the funeral. We all feel terrible that no one could reach her when Poppa died; she was on a trip overseas. She is the adopted Vietnamese daughter Poppa brought from Saigon to assure one of the children in her large family got an education. (Her widowed mother cleaned military apartments.) Poppa seemed to want to make something good of a bad war. He never criticized the war itself—just the politicians who were running it. After she moved away, Jane telephoned Poppa every Sunday and visited often. Ruth always called Poppa "Trimble" (his full name was William Trimble Ezzard), and Jane named her oldest son for him. Trimble Kaleq Chang graduated from MIT and went on to medical school though the Vietnamese grandmother he never knew could neither read nor write.

Poppa was awarded a Purple Heart and a Silver Star during his military career, but we all knew he felt Jane was his finest wartime legacy. He was of that Greatest Generation, scarred by war experiences he never mentioned, bound to his fellow soldiers, but never losing his connection to his North Georgia farm even when he had to spend so many years away from it. He once wrote of the character of the men who went to war from the Southern Appalachians: "The best combat soldiers are men born and reared in the out of doors…they take the weather as it comes; they are never lost, night or day. These are traits not found in men from the populated areas as they are found in men from the hills."[9]

---

[9] A. J. Ritchie, *Sketches of Rabun County History 1819–1948* (Lakemont GA: Copple House Books, 1948) 376.

The week before he died when John and I were at his bedside, he whispered in a delirious moment to John, "Get away from the door, the Germans are coming."

As I think about Poppa, a man of few words, I value many memorable conversations I had with him, but it is a silly one that sticks in my mind. It is symbolic of a trait I always admired—Poppa's ability to accept others as they are, without judgment. He was never critical of my juggling career and children, or of my preference for golf with John over snapping beans with the women when we visited the farm. I especially remember a particular conversation we had during a visit when our three children were young.

After dinner at the rock house, I asked Poppa to tell us about his time in Germany with Elvis Presley. We knew Elvis was a member of the army unit Poppa commanded; he had mentioned to us before that because Elvis spent his early years in the small town of Tupelo, Mississippi, and roamed its rural environs. Elvis knew something about living outdoors, about rifles and good hunting dogs. Poppa clearly liked his savvy about those things.

"Did he perform any music when he was in the service, Poppa? Did you and Grammy listen to his music later?" No response from Poppa, just a silent smile. "Well, tell us this, at least: did you ever jitterbug to 'You Ain't Nothing But a Hound Dog'?" Poppa smiled even more broadly and repeated what he always said about Elvis (even knowing that in his later career Presley was hardly an example of discipline and clean living): "All I can tell you is this: Elvis was absolutely a model soldier," he said.

It seems a trivial comparison, not one the rest of the Ezzard clan would share. But I keep on thinking that the Elvis era has ended, but never will. And now, the Poppa era at the farm has ended too, but he is with us still every day.

A few weeks after Poppa's death, John and I take a long walk, examining our young vines on our way up the winding gravel road from the barn to inspect our new home rising above them on the hillside. We stop to admire the geese honking overhead as they fly in perfect formation to the pond. We stop in front of the large rocks leading to the front door of our home, still under construction, and look out over the undulating rows of vines clinging to the contours of the land like a colorful weaving. The metal roof on the barn reflects the sunlight, and round bales of hay dot the fields beyond.

"It's our turn," John says, his eyes glistening, as he sweeps one arm towards the horizon as if embracing land and sky, "and we have to make something of it."

Martha and John planting the first vines on the farm.

Martha shows off her favorite Tannat grapes at harvest.

The old dairy barn as it looked when the Ezzards moved to the farm.

The red barn is now the entry to the Ezzard Vineyards at Tiger Mountain.
(Photo credit: Ginny Heckel)

The house in the vineyards that daughter Shelly designed.

Martha's roses mark the end of each row of vines.
(Photo credit: Peter McIntosh)

The farm house where John grew up is made of rock from Tiger Mountain.

Farm legend Coach Arvel Holmes,
who thought Mah-tha should go back to the city

A red winged blackbird lights on the first buds of spring.

John drives the "frost dragon" at dawn to fight a late frost.

The "farm girl" in her yellow truck

A label to match the mountains
(Photo credit: Peter McIntosh)

Daughter Shelly and the award winning labels she designed.

For John, clipping grapes at harvest is the ultimate reward.

Lugs filled with Malbec grapes.

John punching down the cap (grape skins) at fermentation

Seed and Feed Marching Abominables at the "Awakening the Vines" party
(Photo credit: Ginny Heckel)

Artists from the Hambidge Center enjoy a vineyard dinner.

John and his daughter Lisa thin the Petit Manseng.

Granddaughter Georgia O' Farrell takes up pruning.

The Ezzard family gathers every summer at the farm.

Winery partners, John Ezzard and John McMullan, celebrate Tiger Mountain's double gold, best of class at the 2012 Los Angeles International Wine Competition.

Martha and John celebrate the 2012 Red Barn Café opening.

9

Strip Tease in the Vineyard

> Come, come, good wine is a good familiar creature, if it be well used; exclaim no more against it. —Othello, *Act II, scene 3*

I sense that the goodness in wine growing is still in doubt in Rabun County though it's been two years since we put in the first vines. For some, the cultivation of wine grapes is not compatible with religious beliefs.

"But the wine grapes were *your* idea," I tease when I feel neighboring fundamentalist Baptists think me a sinner. "You're not from here," John replies with a grin. Apparently, being a native erases a lot of sin in our small mountain community.

On this particular Sunday afternoon in early June, warmer and more humid than usual, as I go with John to our third vineyard-to-be, I wonder out loud if the church women might come calling again—to recruit me for the women's auxiliary or some such. Never mind that I have already been to early communion at our small Episcopal church in Clayton. Never mind that I did not wear my jeans to communion—though some do and it is perfectly acceptable to our Rabun County priest. If the Methodist church ladies were to visit again, they won't know that I even took some homemade cheese biscuits for the coffee hour. Homemade anything is redeeming. When

John and I strike out in the old pick up truck in our tattered work jeans, it occurs to me that there's no privacy in Tiger even on our hundred-acre farm.

We bump across the creek and up the winding, uneven road to the steep hillside that was once covered with Christmas trees (another Ezzard farm project) where John is determined to plant a new vineyard that he claims will be "above the frost line"—that famous local description for any piece of a slope not at the bottom of the hill. I simply don't get the frost line stuff, especially how a higher vineyard is going to be less prone to suffer a late spring frost. But I was present when Poppa told John not to plant down by the creek—which John did anyhow—but to try planting high on this hillside if he wants to avoid late frost. Poppa was never too serious about the tree farm business, but he enjoyed giving away Christmas trees to poor families in the county who would drop by every holiday season. When they insisted on paying something, he charged them a dollar. Now the hillside has been cleared of the rows of white pines except for some giant ones that serve as its backdrop, trees Poppa planted and let go at the edge of the woods on the mountain.

John and Coach have already laid out fifteen new rows on the hillside, but the posts and trellises have yet to be put in. John hands me a set of post-hole diggers.

Okay, I think to myself—*he's not just my low-tech man; he's my* no-*tech man.*

"Is this a joke or what?" I ask. "There has to be an easier way to do this."

"There is," John says, "but it costs more and think of the great exercise and conditioning we'd miss." I ponder silently how I might be able to get my entire LA Fitness class from Atlanta up here. This work could surely sub for weightlifting. Nevertheless, I watch my husband's demonstration and give it a try. He assigns me a row he says has fewer rocks in the soil and won't be as hard to dig. After I dig holes for three posts, I am dripping in sweat. I look up to see that my husband has dug nine holes and has taken his shirt off. I decide to follow suit, tying my denim shirt around my waist and spraying bug repellent around my bra.

Suddenly I hear a noise that sounds like a motor. I look warily down the road towards the house and start to untie my shirt. John laughs out loud. "Don't be silly," he says. "That's not a car motor—it's a ruffed grouse call."

"A ruffed what?"

"A grouse," he repeats. "Hunters love them. They're game birds that have a ruff around their neck like some member of a royal family; they also have distinctive white markings on their tail feathers that make them look like miniature turkeys. They make that drumming sound, like the revving up of a motor, by cupping and beating their wings in the air."

"Sounds a little like a motorcycle," I reply. "I guess the women of the church wouldn't be arriving on cycles." I had a vision of what a stir it would create if the church women came calling and found me topless (so to speak) in the vineyard. *"Did you hear about that Ezzard woman?"* they'd say at the local quilting club. *"She has a wild side just as we thought, leaving the good doctor to work all week in the city—and now she's doing a strip tease in the vineyard."*

Of course, I know I will always have a defender at the quilting club in John's cousin, Janie P., whose house we can see from this particular hillside. Family loyalty is her finest trait, and I know she would defend me even if I were running around stark naked in the vineyards.

As the afternoon sun beats down on me, I began to get in the rhythm of the post-hole digging. I hum a few bars of "Summertime—and the livin' is easy...." This is not easy work, but there is something rewarding about seeing these perfect rows cling to the contours of the land. John and I dig deep holes in order to set one trellis post for every four vines. How does he know to space them that way? Dennis Horton, of course. Worrying about possible bug bites, I put my shirt back on after another hour of digging and stop to rest. Blisters have formed on my hands beneath my work gloves.

A soft wind blows across the hayfield below the new vineyard and makes waves in the tall grasses that flow like the movements of a symphony. John walks quietly down to the big rock where I'm resting. "Look," he whispers, pointing toward the waving grass below the new vineyard site, "it's a mother deer and her fawn." The two deer, paying no heed to the humans toiling above them, jump and scamper in the field. They have the right idea, playing and enjoying their day in the country. But a country day for my husband is more enjoyable in the end if there is work to be admired, progress toward his dream vineyards becoming reality. The jury is out on how much of this work I will enjoy—but I am learning that the work can be invigorating even when it's sticky and sweaty and buggy. At least there is this: the church women did not come calling, only the graceful and carefree mother deer and her little fawn.

We load the old pick-up as the sun sinks behind the mountain. My shoulders ache, and I have a beauty of a blister on my right hand. Still, John is happy with the rows we finished, ready now to set posts with Coach, and I feel exhilarated from the work. I will drive back to the city tonight and must hurry to the farmhouse to pack, my Sunday night drudgery. One thing is for sure: I'm *not* going to roll out of bed in the morning for my 6:30 aerobics class—convenient as it is, just downstairs in my Colony House condo building.

Farm weekends come and go, and new challenges in the vineyards continue. We dust Sevin on the Japanese beetles that visit in droves in July, trying to make lace of our shiny, healthy grape leaves overnight. It's a pretty benign repellent, but we soon realize if we don't get the stuff directly on the beetles, they'll live on and multiply the next day. John puts in calls to both Horton and the Rabun County extension agent to discuss the beetle problem. There must be a better way to eliminate these pests. He begins to investigate sprays that are systemic—insecticides, in fact. I shudder at the thought, always wanting our vineyards to be as chemical-free as possible, but John decides it's necessary to try one of them.

Though our house is not finished, the children drop in for their farm visits over the summer months—a great time for picking berries and fishing in the pond. We eat lots of freshly caught blue gill and bass from the pond. John cleans and filets the fish on an old metal table in back of the farmhouse, a thoroughly gory process that includes headless fish bodies flopping around. All three of the grown children, including the two daughters, are anxious to try their hand at the filleting.

Lisa is the last to leave from the series of summer family visits. It's the first week of August, and while she and I are having coffee one morning, we look out the window to see John in tattered hat and old goggles, tying a pink checkered dish towel around his nose as he hops on the tractor, shiny blue sprayer attached.

Lisa runs for her camera, and we both giggle at the sight. I know John has decided to spray an insecticide to get rid of the beetles. In the afternoon, Lisa and I go to the Reeves Hardware and buy John his first spray mask—though the dishtowel certainly offers more character.

"Is this type of harmful spray a one-time thing," I ask John over dinner that evening, "or are we going to face this every summer?"

"I don't know yet," he responds. "The application of this spray this early in the growing season seems to be standard practice in east coast vineyards. We're not harvesting any grapes yet, but even if we were, this is plenty of time before harvest for it to be safe."

Lisa, who writes poetry and speaks French fluently, has just returned from a year of teaching at the University of Bordeaux as part of her graduate studies. She tells us we *have* to plant roses at the end of each row of vines, an ancient custom in French vineyards and indeed throughout Europe and a practice in much of California wine country today.

"The roses are a harbinger of disease, Mom," she says. "They will attract the beetles first, so you'll get fair warning when they are coming." We soon learn that modern vineyard cultivation techniques are way ahead of roses on predicting and preventing disease. But I can tell that roses are part of vineyard aesthetics in every wine book I pick up—and I resolve that they will be part of our vineyard look too.

We drive to the airport, and I give Lisa a hug. "I'm going to give Dad some rose bushes for our anniversary this year," I assure her. "Maybe he'll do the same at your urging. It will be like the old song, 'You Don't Bring Me Flowers'—just rose bushes. And the next time you come, you'll be able to sleep in our new home."

"And I can't wait to taste some Tiger wine," she says.

"One step at a time," I reply. "I can't wait to see our first harvest next year."

10

The Connoisseur Bear

> Lord, Lord, if you can't help me, please don't help that bear... —*Appalachian ballad*

After three years of waiting for our first harvest and for our very own home on the farm, it all happens at once. Our bedroom, with floor-to-ceiling windows, faces east, and we wake after our first night to a stunning orange and pink sunrise.

I pad around barefoot from room to room with a first cup of coffee, soaking in views I've seen before but never all at once. Morning sun sends streaks of light dancing across the dining room floor and walls from the clerestory windows above. I can see the red barn, just as planned, from my kitchen stove. I hurry upstairs with my coffee to take in the view from the windows that wrap all the way around the corners of the library tower. I admire the ridgelines of the familiar mountains beyond the vineyards and the hayfields—the graceful twin peaks of Raven's Wing and the distant knob that is Rabun Bald, which our family has climbed many times. I've already suggested to John that we look for a ladder tall enough to reach the high clerestory windows and paint it purple for fun—so our family and visitors will be enticed to climb up and view the pond. He rolled his eyes on that one, but maybe he'll come around. Right now, we can only see the very top of the willow tree on the pond's edge from the library.

I have to pinch myself that our home—the house that Shelly built—is reality at last. I wish she were here to celebrate the first morning with me. Like most parents, we have given much to our children, but when I think of the daily joy Shelly's unique design will bring us the rest of our lives, I know I can never repay her. I also know she feels creating it for us is her reward.

It's just past 7 A.M. By the time I get back downstairs, John is headed out the door in his worn boots and stained hat, walking towards his tractor as if punching some farm clock in the sky. Farm and vineyard work are so unstructured for me that I fumble with my day's beginning. I'm accustomed to the demands of meetings and memos—and in my lawyer days, to recording endless billable hours; at the newspaper, daily deadlines organize my day. At the farm, I'm on my own to create the day's checkpoints. On the other hand, John reports in early each morning to his Tiger Mountain earth and to his vines, with a list in his head of the day's demands: suckers to pull off the young vines, trellis wires to tighten, a farm road to scrape before it erodes, fertilizer to spread.

Though I long to go outside, our new home feels very outside—and creating order inside is my immediate challenge. I fret over the pieces of furniture that simply don't "go" while admiring how perfectly my tall copper lamps and large square porous marble coffee table look in the living room, to say nothing of a couple of dark wood antique pieces that are a perfect contrast with the bleached oak floors. I tote my two newly purchased pieces of contemporary art from room to room to decide where they will show best—black and white grid patterns so intricately painted as to look like weavings that float to eternity. They are by Georgia artist friend Annette Cone Skelton, founder of the Museum of Contemporary Art in Atlanta; they speak to my feminist side as if they were essays about rhythm, repetition, and redemption. The red wall in the kitchen-family area is perfect for them I finally decide. I chuckle to myself when I think about John's reaction to the red wall when Shelly and I first suggested it. He decided it was as much fun as we thought in the end, especially when Shelly said, "Dad, you and Mom are simply not pastel people."

Of course, John and I have completely different taste in art, so the pieces we own are an eclectic mix—his favorite a western landscape by Charles Berninghouse, a Santa Fe artist. He has already decided it should go on the living room side of the three-way fireplace. Not for long, I resolve. I have a bolder art piece in mind for that spot, the first thing you see when you come in our front door. I am saving one side of the fireplace wall for a special painting by Shelly—when she can find time to finish it.

John teasingly calls my latest "grid" art pieces "the car seats," though he is soon touting them to all who come to visit—stunning as they are on the red wall and as much as he likes and admires the artist. Among our art from Colorado, I love the painting Shelly selected of two giant coffee cups by a Hispanic artist she knows. One is red, the other blue, on a gold background; the painting, which covers most of one wall, pulls the entire family room together. John agrees with me that any new art we purchase ought to be works of Georgia or regional artists if possible. I already have my eye on an elegant Blue Ridge mountain potter, Ben Owen III, and on an artist, Gil Martin, who paints contemporary works and who makes his paints from the earth.

The furnishings and art will have to evolve—I know that. Even as is, I can't wait to share our new home with our friends. I begin to make a list for a Sunday brunch that will include close neighbors and my newspaper editor and his wife who led us to our builder, Winfred McKay. In addition to McKay and his wife, we invite the handful of North Georgia craftsmen whose talents helped make our home unique. It is perfect that our daughter Shelly, who designed our vineyard home, is visiting. This brunch will be our thank you and housewarming.

When summer arrives, all three children and the three young grandchildren come to pick blueberries, fish in the pond, and help christen our new home. It's mid-August when they come, and our red grapes are already undergoing *veraison*, turning from green to purple on the vine. (I record that miracle with dozens of photos. I especially love the clusters when they first turn and are briefly shades of both green and purple.)

Another visitor pays a surprise visit to the vineyards as we approach our first harvest—a connoisseur black bear. John runs into the house the morning after the children arrive to announce that something is eating our grapes—something big. He knows right away it's a bear because of the bear scat in the vineyard. We all rush out to see. But the vines, to our surprise, are not mauled or broken; rather, there are empty stems on some rows as if each grape had been hand selected for tasting. John tells us black bears are protected in Georgia except for a brief late fall hunting season, but he says state wildlife officials will try to trap them if they are threatening human life or destroying a crop. He puts in a phone call to the regional mountain wildlife office—and sure enough, before the day is out, a truck pulling a long tubular metal trap arrives at the farm. After some discussion of possible sites for it, John and the wildlife officers decide to place it in a cove above the house near the old Concord eating grapes that the bear has also sampled.

That night, I tell John it's ridiculous to think that we'll really catch a bear. The next morning at sunrise, John sneaks quietly out of the house while the rest of us are still asleep and hides at the edge of the woods to observe the trap. Sure enough, a huge black bear appears to investigate it—the smell of the fish bait, horrible to us, is inviting to him. John watches him start into the trap twice, he later reports, only to back out. The metal door will not slam shut until the bear disturbs the bait at the other end; that's so the trap door won't injure the bear going in. The third time, the bear can't resist the bait at the far end and the door slams down.

John races to the house and we all jump out of bed and head up the hill to the trap, most of us in our pajamas and whatever sweat shirts we can find. The grandchildren, two four-year-olds and a three-year old, eyes as big as saucers, squeal with a mixture of excitement and fear when they hear the growling of the angry bear. As we all gather around the trap to view our connoisseur bear, whom John Jr. names "Cabernet," my husband suddenly starts singing an old ballad about a preacher and a bear. Though John plays the piano, he is not blessed with a great singing voice. The tune is a little hard to follow, but the words are hysterical to those of us, including me, who have never heard the mountain ballad—one that relatives tell me later has a number of versions. The version John bellows out about a preacher returning from quail hunting and running into a bear is memorable:

> The preacher turned his eyes to the sky
> And these are the words he prayed:
> "Oh Lord, you delivered Daniel from the lions' den
> Jonah from the belly of the whale, Amen!
> The Hebrew children from the fiery furnace
> Now the good book do declare
> Lord, Lord, if you can't help me
> Please don't help that bear!"

"Cabernet" offered background growling during the song, and the grandchildren giggled as we all broke into laughter at John's impromptu performance. Soon Coach and the neighbors came to see the bear—then the wildlife officials we'd called. One of the officers I'd befriended when they set the trap up is Lonnie Speed, a pleasant, burly man with a thick Southern accent.

"Lonnie," I ask, as the wildlife officers prepare to haul the bear and the trap away, "do you think this bear grew up on Tiger Mountain?" I had hiked many mornings alone on a makeshift trail above our house, and it never crossed my mind that I might run into a bear.

"I do, ma'am," he replied, his accent soft and melodic. "I believe he's just a local bear."

I tug at John's arm. "Did you hear that? A local bear and we're moving him from his native home."

"Local bear or not," John replies, "he's worth about $1,500 of our first harvest." Officials explain that they will sedate the bear and tag him before releasing him into a remote area at Rabun Bald mountain about twenty-five miles away. The tag will help them track him should he return to nearby farms. Young black bears like this one are territorial, Lonnie tells us, and there's a chance we'll see him again—but hopefully not during our harvest. A neighbor takes pictures for us when "Cabernet" is set free at Rabun Bald, so the grandchildren will know nothing bad happened to him. The bear episode is the stuff of many a show and tell when they return home.

After the children and grandchildren leave, John gets serious about measuring grape sugars as they creep steadily upward towards the end of August. With our new refractometer, a gismo that looks like a miniature microscope, we run around the vineyards every evening taking sugar samples. We test one variety at a time, picking at random individual grapes until we have almost a cupful. Then, we mash them with a wooden pestle and pour a little juice on the glass "door" of the refractometer, looking through it at the sugar "scale," which is similar to a thermometer, but in "brix," the measuring unit for all fruit sugars including grapes. John says ideally we want 22 to 24 brix, but if the grape seeds are browning and the grapes taste good, we can pick at a minimum of 19 or 20 brix—especially if some of the grapes start to split or turn soft.

John has already contracted with Dennis Horton for the purchase of our grapes this first harvest. He assures me we will save some grapes to make a little wine for fun. He has already arranged for a refrigerated truck to come to the farm when he gives the signal that the grapes are ripe enough to harvest. John tentatively retains a crew of area agricultural workers to help us pick. Now, he's having misgivings about being forced to pick all of the grape varieties at one time although we have only red grapes mature enough for harvesting. "I won't do this again," he says the evening after he returns from riding all night to Virginia with the truck driver and his precious first harvest. "Different varieties ripen at different times. The Malbec should have been picked already; they are getting soft—but the Cabernet Franc are barely ripe enough."

One day during the harvest, a neighbor with a home at Tiger Mountain Orchard stops by to talk to John. Bill Stack, an Atlanta lawyer, and his wife, Leckie, have been making apple wine on their scenic farm, where pears, persimmons, apples and berries grow in abundance. He's admired John's vineyards before but admits he was skeptical that the fine wine grapes, *vinifera*, could thrive in North Georgia. He suggests John save not just a few grapes but enough for a couple of barrels to experiment with winemaking. John already owns some barrels, two of which are French oak and were gifts from his colleagues when he left Denver. (That was quite a sight—barrels hauled into the Cherry Hills Country Club—

and John's doctor friends shaking their heads in both envy and disbelief that John would leave a thriving practice in his fifties to plant wine grapes in the South.) A couple of other barrels are used American oak John purchased on a lark. He readily agrees to Bill's suggestion and is excited about trying to make wine from our first harvest. The two decide later to crush the grapes John saves—mostly Cabernet Franc, Tannat, and Norton—with an old apple press discovered in the apple-packing house at neighboring Tiger Mountain Orchard. Our farmer friend Bob Massee, the orchard manager, lets us use it.

I go over to the warehouse with my camera to witness the process. John is purple from head to toe, and juice is splattered all over his clothes as multiple small batches of grapes are crushed for a good six or seven hours with the most primitive equipment. It is a scene from medieval times—though I'm surprised at how well the two new "vintners" have figured out the process, purchased the proper wine yeast and other necessities for wine making. The Stacks have a ground-level basement with a driveway that can accommodate a truck, so the plan, after the juice ferments on the skins in some borrowed metal vats, is to press it in the old apple press, ridding the juice of the skins, pump it into John's barrels and haul it to Bill's basement for aging. Despite their makeshift equipment, they have studied, like two mad chemists, the entire process, measuring alcohol levels, acid, and sugars and exactly how much sulfite to add after fermentation to kill any bacteria.

Meanwhile, at Horton Vineyards, Dennis is pleased with the quality of the grapes he purchased from John. He calls one day to ask John how in the world he got such "black" Tannat juice. "Those Tannat vines are identical to yours, Dennis," John replies. "Sharon ordered the plants for me." Dennis declares his Tannat have never produced juice with such deep, purple color.

"I guess it's all about our Tiger *terroir*," I tell John, in my wine person know-it-all voice.

11

Turning a Creamery into a Winery

> Time in the bottle, time in the barrel, time on the vine.... The best part of the whole lengthy process is when we get to drink. —*Joy Sterling*[10]

In the following months, we take friends over to Bill's basement to barrel taste. When Shelly and Brian come for a visit, six months after we have pumped our very first wine into three barrels, we can't wait to take them to taste. Brian, like his father, collects fine wines and has by far the best palate in our family. He never comments on a wine that is mediocre or worse. He doesn't need to—we all know what his sipping in silence means.

John gives the four of us glasses and pulls some of the rich, deep red juice out of the Cabernet Franc barrel using his new toy, a long tubular "wine thief." Brian tastes and doesn't say a word, then asks to taste again.

"Damn," he exclaims, "this is some of the best Cabernet Franc I've ever had."

"Uh-oh," John replies with a wide grin, "maybe we really will have wine that's good enough to sell."

---

[10] Joy Sterling and Amy Katz, *Vineyard* (New York: Simon & Schuster, 1998).

Over the following months, John and Bill share stories of friends' positive reactions to their barrel tastings. (Okay, so a few people didn't like the Norton.) But one afternoon, we four taste the three barrels seriously and multiple times—in addition to the Cabernet Franc, the Norton, Malbec, and Tannat are excellent too. Giddy and euphoric, we decide to go for it—open our own winery. We agree to contribute equal and modest amounts of money for the most basic equipment.

When we made that leap, had we perhaps drunk too much wine? In the weeks that follow, John and I have days when we wonder about our decision—but on more days than not, we can hardly contain our excitement about making wine from the vineyard we have nourished for four years. It's as if our vines, now looking healthy and vibrant, are our babies finally beginning to take off by themselves.

While I'm still spending long hours at my newspaper post in Atlanta, fighting the traffic late on Friday evening to get to the farm, John and Bill are moving big vats and air cooling equipment into the old Ezzard creamery building (on the historic Highway 441 just down the road from the farmhouse) in preparation for our first commercial vintage. Bill surfs the Internet for second-hand equipment while John is still tending every vine individually. John and Bill purchase some new American oak barrels from World Cooperage. American oak is less expensive than the French oak, and they decide the American oak barrels will work well for fermenting the red wines. Bill orders a shiny new European-made red crusher de-stemmer as well as a small wine press.

Summer arrives, and Georgia is in its second year of a record drought. We have finally figured out that dry is good for our grapes, even those varieties John planted specifically because he knew they would withstand the humid climate. In Tiger, we go thirty-five days without a drop of rain, and John begins to worry about his youngest vines whose leaves start to curl. The roots of the established vines will struggle deep in the earth to get water and that stress will give us more intense juice, but new vines can't do that. It rains a little in Clayton; it rains a little in Tallulah Gorge; it rains some at Lake Rabun, but not in Tiger. My flower garden is pathetic and the grass is turning brown. In Atlanta and other parts of North Georgia there are outdoor watering restrictions, but we are lucky to be on well water for which no such constraints apply. When I arrive at the farm on a Friday evening, John lets me know that Coach and I are part of his Saturday watering team—we'll all have to pull hoses from the well—up and down eight rows of the youngest of his vines. He promises us dinner at The Dillard House, just up the road, which serves authentic Southern fare. (John Dillard is among the few locals who encouraged John's wine grape venture from the beginning.)

Our son, John Jr., now living in the D.C. area, decides to come for a long weekend to help out. It is hot and heavy work; by early afternoon, we look like the crew from Gilligan's Island—we are splattered with dirt, and our clothes are drenched in water from the hoses. A neighbor drives up to the vineyard with his windshield wipers on—we assume from the car wash. He reports excitedly that it is raining up the road in Mountain City. After our eight hours of toiling with our primitive irrigation system, it makes me mad to think it might not have been necessary. But, rain showers never come that evening to Tiger—nor do they for another six days.

John talks to his favorite farmer friend Bob Massee at Tiger Mountain Orchards. "I never thought, Bob, that I'd be wishing for moisture for wine grapes when I'm usually fighting too much of it." Bob assures him it won't happen often in these parts and shakes his head about the effects of the extreme drought on his apple trees—like John, worrying about those that are newly planted.

In August there are only a few sporadic showers, and it stays bone dry clear though September harvest. Instead of being forced to pick all of our grapes at one time as John had done the previous fall to take them to Horton's in Virginia, we have a chance to decide which varieties of grapes to pick when—knowing those decisions will be crucial to the ripeness of the grapes and the quality of our initial commercial vintage.

I take some vacation time to help with the harvest.

John comes racing in the house one evening the first week of September as if sirens were sounding in the vineyards. He yells, "The Malbec are ripe, the Malbec are going to fall apart if we don't pick them tomorrow. Call everyone we know. We need help picking in the morning."

I head to my messy desk by the telephone in my study wishing I'd been more organized about recording contacts for all of the local folks who mentioned from time to time to John or me how much they'd like to help pick grapes at harvest. Of course I can call our good friends, the Hatchers and the Kronsnobles; Bob Hatcher and Jeff Kronsnoble have helped John before. I can call my photographer friend and fellow hiker, Peter McIntosh, who lives nearby. (Peter and I trekked together for a newspaper series, "Five Great Hikes in North Georgia.") I find the names of some local doctors and nurses John knows scribbled in our phone directory. And—who else? All of a sudden, I come upon our St. James Episcopal Church Directory. Ah-ha!—a lot of our parishioners are outdoorsy types, and many of them love wine. Some are retirees who aren't on full-time work schedules either. Those calls prove fruitful, and John reminds me to call Travis Barnes as well. Travis is a beloved, retired Methodist minister with a great sense of humor. His wife, Kathy, is a columnist for the local newspaper; they are some of our favorite Tiger neighbors. When I phone Travis to ask what he's planning to do tomorrow he responds that he plans to minister to some folks in the nursing home—then he pauses: "But the Lord says when your neighbor needs help, you should help him. I'll be there. What time?"

We welcome eight or nine people to the Malbec vineyard—they all show up before 9 A.M. to help us pick. John goes up and down the rows instructing our helpers to throw on the ground any clusters that are "mushy." Few are, despite John's frenzy about the thin-skinned Malbec. We break for lunch at the picnic table under the old Yates apple tree. I bring lemonade, promising to save a bottle of our first Malbec vintage, another year and a half away, for each of our volunteer pickers. Cameras click, and the conversation and laughter in the vineyards tell me this is more fun than hiring a crew of pickers, but will friends and neighbors want to return time and time again?

"Once you plant it, a grapevine isn't like sweet corn that you can decide not to plant again in the spring," John tells some of our Episcopal church friends who have dubbed themselves "the parish pickers." "A grapevine is like eternity—it's forever," John says. He often tells me that tending the vineyards is reminiscent of the dairy farm when he was young because the vines, like the cows, never go away. They require care in all seasons of the year.

After such a convivial picking time, we decide with our partners to stage a first harvest party and invite a larger group to pick grapes and enjoy a picnic lunch a few weeks later. Gathered again under the old Yates apple tree at two tables, the group of local wine lovers listen as John and Bill talk a little bit about the varieties of grapes and the wine making process in which they are engaged. They explain the requirements for being a farm winery, the most important of which is that at least half the grapes must be grown in the county. We promise that when we release our first wine, we'll invite everyone to taste. This time I've picked up some aged artisan cheeses from a gourmet market in Atlanta, and we share some of Horton's Norton with a group of twenty at the picnic lunch. Some pick only an hour or two, and others stay all day.

Long, intense days follow as each variety ripens to picking time. Bill and John spend twelve or more hours at a time in the small creamery-turned-winery building, ending with the crushing of each of the six varieties of red grapes in our vineyards. Then, the juice and skins go into open tanks where the fermenting juice must sit on the skins for about ten days. John consults with Dennis on the phone about several issues, and he and Bill measure precise amounts of yeast to juice and take turns punching down the "cap"—the skins and seeds that float to the top and, amazingly, form a semi-hard crust. We've already learned that we should skim the seeds off as best we can lest our wines turn out to be too "herbal."

"The fermenting wine emits carbon dioxide, and if we don't punch the cap down," John says, wielding a new boat oar for the task, "these tanks could explode."

"Isn't there a piece of equipment made especially for punching down the cap?" I ask.

"Yep," he replies, "but this works just as well." I remember visiting a large California winery once where huge automated machines rolled though the production room lowering and raising vertical metal poles with round bottoms to pierce the big fermentation tanks. I recall also that some wineries advertise that they "hand punch," so this tedious process may be a plus for our boutique winery image (although I'm not too sure about the boat oar approach). John volunteers to punch down a couple of times at night since we live so close to the winery. He goes back to punch down "the cap" on the fermenting juice at about 10:00, comes home and sets the alarm for 2:00 A.M. the first night, but we are so tired we don't hear it go off. When he hops up at 6:00 A.M. and goes to check on the fermenting vats of wine, his worst fears are realized. There are grape skins hanging from the ceiling of the small creamery building, and juice covers the equipment and the floor. Hours and hours of cleanup follow, but the explosion makes a colorful harvest story. The two vats filled to the brim are the ones that exploded. The lesson? Fill the open vats no more than two thirds full from now on.

We've got that.

After pushing big vats and heavy barrels around in the cramped creamery building for a few months, John and Bill decide it's time to build a barrel room behind the creamery. We all agree that it can double as our tasting room. Knowing already how difficult it is to cool a building without putting in super-expensive equipment, we consult our friend and house-builder, Winfred McKay, about digging into the hill so the barrel room can be structured more like a cave, for temperature control purposes—though I am outvoted on my preference for a flat contemporary roof. The Stacks and John want the roof to be gabled like the creamery building in front; but there will at least be glass on the gables in front and back—and a view of the top of Tiger Mountain from the back gable window. From the back of the new barrel room, only the gable shows above the ground—the rest in built into the hill.

With the excavation into the hillside comes geological confirmation that our soils at Tiger are pretty ideal for European *vinifera*. The exposed strata of dirt and rock, shades of deep rust and gray, reveal layers of ancient degenerated granite, thin ribbons of red clay, a little sand and some dark, loamy soil in places. John is especially pleased to confirm his theory that degenerated granite makes up such a large part of the soils at Tiger Mountain, somewhat akin to the wine-growing region of Bordeaux.

John and Bill hone their winemaking skills over the winter while our new barrel room is being constructed. Their plan is to let the red wines age for more than a year (we have no white wines at this point) before bottling our first commercial release. They hire a couple of workers to help them rack the wines in winter and spring. ("Racking" is the process of pumping the wine out of the barrels periodically and washing each barrel to remove the "leas"—any remaining sediment—then pumping the wine back. It's a labor-intensive task.) John says racking should be done three times in the life of a fermenting red wine.

John and Bill begin to analyze acids and sugars, measure pH levels and talk to experts and anyone else with a shred of knowledge about winemaking. They have already read stacks of books recommended to them from various sources. What the two of them don't finish on weekends in preparation for the first bottling, John does during the week with the help of some part-time workers. Meanwhile, Bill spends much of his time in his Atlanta law office figuring out how to get federal and state license approvals for our new winery.

Finally, one day more than a year after the second harvest (we sold most of our first harvest to Horton), John and Bill call Leckie and me to "officially" taste their three best red grape blends. We all prefer one that is fruity and spicy and, we think, a bit unusual too. After some brainstorming, it's easy to agree on a name for the five-grape blend: it will be Rabun Red, named, of course, after our home Rabun County.

"The folks who have places at Lake Rabun are going to love this," John exclaims. "They won't be able to resist our Rabun Red to display and serve in their lake homes."

Our benchmark wine, ready to release after fourteen months of barrel aging (though future red vintages may barrel age longer) is made primarily of Cabernet Franc and Norton although it also has Malbec, Tannat, and Mourvedre in it. We all raise a toast beside our shiny new bottling machine, which will bottle four bottles at a time of our locally grown and produced Rabun Red, our very first Tiger Mountain Vineyards wine.

12

Erotic Tease: The Tiger Mountain Label

Where there is no wine, there is no love. —*Euripides*

We confer with county officials about a farm winery license that will allow us to pour wine in our tasting room and sell it retail as well. A "farm winery" for our conservative rural area has a nicer ring than booze and beer. The wording of the ordinance that is agreed upon declares, as we knew it would, that at least 50 percent of the fruit must be locally grown to qualify as a farm winery. Not a problem—our wines are 100 percent Rabun County grown.

Come late summer and another harvest, complete with a small harvest party, we get more and more excited about how our barrel room-tasting room is coming together. But—wait! We don't yet have a label for our Tiger Mountain wine. That indeed turns out to be a big challenge for the four of us to agree upon.

John and I propose a vertical label design, an idea we got from our good friends and wine collectors in Colorado, Alan and Katie Fox. They pointed out an eye catching vertical label on a bottle of California wine from their cellar. John and I told Shelly about it later—and she began to play with various designs.

There is the age-old question, of course, about whether labels sell wine. A unique label, I argue, can attract a buyer to a new wine, but, of course, the quality of what's in the bottle keeps that buyer coming back. As John and I look in our own modest wine cellar at label designs, nothing, of course, is more elegant than Chateau d'Yquem's understated gold and cream label. But we are not famous and we are not French. Then, there are the irreverent Bonny Doon labels like "Big House Red," which depicts an Alcatraz prison escape. We want to capture our Blue Ridge Mountain feel, but we don't want to look like moonshine, muscadine wine, or hard cider.

In our cellar, we pick out a bottle of Imagery wine, from the Sonoma winery owned by (but separate from) Benzinger. Imagery commissions original art labels with only one requirement: that a Parthenon image, symbol of the Benzinger estate, be part of every design, either prominent or hidden. I tell John about an article I'd read once giving the history of Chateau Mouton Rothschild's coveted labels and wines. The revered French wine of the Pauillac, Rothchild wines display collector art labels that date to the early twentieth century and include original commissioned works by Pablo Picasso and Andy Warhol.

What we are looking for is something fresh and earthy, a label that cries out *I'm neither Napa nor Bordeaux, just saucy, boldly American, a wine of the Blue Ridge Mountains.* Shelly sketches several ideas, but the one we like best is the vertical profile of the mountain against a colorful sky and a stripe on the opposite side, with Tiger Mountain Vineyards in bold, clean lettering below it, also vertical on the bottle. Shelly suggests we use the same design but with three different colors for each wine we produce, an idea we all like. When viewed horizontally, the design is obviously the outline of our mystical, crooked mountain. There is something earthy yet whimsical about it. But it turns out to tease when viewed vertically—not as a mountain profile (which it is horizontally) but as possibly a woman's breast—shhhh! (As if making wine commercially in our conservative mountain county isn't already radical enough.) We laugh—you have to strain to make the erotic connection, and for those who do, who knows, it might be another factor to entice a new buyer.

We all agree on bold, bright hues for the labels. The Rabun Red will have a purple sky above the mountain outline; the mountain will be chartreuse and the stripe yellow. Our first vintage of Rabun Red is indeed a lively dry wine, with deep cherry flavors up front and a slightly peppery finish, a characteristic of the Norton. The label reflects that freshness. It's easy for us to come up with different colors for the other wines—colors that speak to the character of each. For the Cabernet Franc, Shelly chooses a deep maroon mountain, with a mustard sky above and a dark purple stripe down the side. That intriguing richness of hues projects the French varietal's dark berry flavors and herbal tinged bouquet. The Norton colors can be brighter, making a statement about a fruity American wine with a lot of spice to it—a red mountain against a yellow sky, complemented by an apple green stripe. Though it's possible to detect hints of chocolate or tobacco in it, Norton is a rich, hearty dry wine any American might choose to drink with a thick steak.

Our back label will simply tell the story of our winery's beginnings and of the two families' deep respect for the land at Tiger that we hope our wines reflect. The back label, for better or worse, will be the same for all of our wines, at least for now.

Bill figures out the federal label approval process and sends in Shelly's drawings and the wording on our back label. Under the name of the wine on the front label will be simply "Georgia red wine." But one of our labels is sent back immediately from the Federal Alcohol and Tobacco Tax and Trade Bureau, asking us to fulfill the "import requirements." When Bill calls to find out what in the world that means, he discovers that some federal bureaucrat thought our wine was made in the old *Soviet* Georgia. No question, the state of Georgia has a long way to go to be recognized as a producer of fine wines.

Bill and I are still racing to Atlanta for the workweek, so John and Leckie carry out the bulk of preparation for the opening of our tasting room. John gets the old creamery building painted to match the outside of the new light gray stucco structure we built to house barrels and serve as our first tasting room. There is a bit of nostalgia for John and me in covering up "Ezzard," the bold black letters that marked the vegetable and berry stand for which the creamery building was best known when Poppa was alive. Leckie brings in giant flower arrangements, mostly native wildflowers and perennials, perfect for our earthy image. The flowers from Leckie's garden are stunning colors, combined with some Queen Anne's lace from our hayfields and long canes of bright yellow broom that grow on the roadside.

I get a Tiger Mountain Vineyards sign made in Atlanta to hang on the corner of the creamery building, and we order a couple of large, vertical banners, replicas of our labels that we can put on metal stands inside or outside. With gourmet cheeses and our new wine glasses arranged on a huge round wood tabletop (supported by three barrels), our party is set. Our tasting room opening draws almost one hundred people, including the good friends of both families—and we count it a great success, since our publicity, except for a feature story in the *Clayton Tribune*, is limited to mailed postcards of our Rabun Red label image and some flyers tacked up around town.

We decide to keep the tasting room open only on weekends and agree that Stacks will take one weekend and Ezzards the other since we have no tasting room "staff" at this point.

Soon, though, we find our first winery administrator, Judy Ruth, a retired Episcopal church administrator—the perfect transition, according to Judy, among whose endearing qualities is her keen sense of humor and ready quips that foil any tensions that arise. She's an organizer and a stickler for bookkeeping and willing to work part time. Fortunately for us, the Ruths had rented the rock farmhouse a while back, so she's just up the hill from the winery.

Our bottles and labels arrive, and we are ecstatic. There's only one problem: where is the bottling, corking, sealing, and labeling crew?

You're looking at it," John cracks.

"I'll call Judy," I say. "She'll have some ideas about helpers."

Sure enough, Judy finds some neighbors and friends, going so far as to call on a few members of her quilting club to show up.

John, Bill, Leckie, and I take turns with the manual corker, which corks one bottle at a time.

"You can give up weight lifting," I tell the friends in my city aerobics class, "and just come up and help us cork our new wine."

There's plenty of laughter, but no takers.

At the last minute, we decide to add a narrow tiger stripe just below the capsule top of our Bordeaux-shaped bottles. It's not too much "tiger," which we shied away from at the start of the label discussions, but the right, understated touch of tiger!

The problem? Instead of having the stripe incorporated into the "capsule" that covers the cork and bottleneck that we secure with a heated sealing device, we'll have to wrap each tiger stripe on hundreds of bottles by hand. We put some lively CDs in the boom box, grab some chicken and veggie wraps and chips for lunches, and call in the troops for another labeling challenge.

As it turns out, all of our first vintages, on the release calendar already, get the hand-wrapped treatment. *Never again* we vow, knowing that having the stripe incorporated in the caps when they are made will solve the problem in the future, even though there's a hefty one-time expense for doing so.

When it comes time to bottle and wrap the tiger stripes on the Norton, Judy is first to volunteer to help, and with good reason. Before our first harvest, Judy's husband, John, retired from the Federal Aviation Administration but best known in our community for his dedication as a volunteer fireman, had helped John in the Norton vines. John gave him one of the first six Tiger Mountain Vineyards hats we had, and he wore it with pride. Sadly, he died of pancreatic cancer before we harvested our first Norton. When I walk past those rows of Norton beside the road on my way to visit the farm pond, I can still see and hear John R. chuckle, happily wielding his clippers on our undisciplined American grape to which he devoted a couple of seasons. The in-your-face Norton, with its canes growing in all directions can best be tamed by even-tempered, happy souls like John Ruth—I'm sure of it.

After his death, Judy quietly asks John if she can spread her John's ashes in the Norton vineyard.

"Of course," John replies. "Our Norton vines will forever need John Ruth."

John tells me Judy wants to be alone in this sacred remembrance. We well understand, but I am in tears over the beautiful symbolism that this gentle, unselfish soul, a dedicated community servant and an avid vegetable gardener, a fun-loving man with a constant twinkle in his eyes, is now part of the land and the vines we love.

The women of our small St. James Episcopal Church who design, quilt, or embroider the vestments and altar cloths, make robes for the priest and cloths for the alter with grape designs and harvest themes. Needless to say, their intricate work is dedicated to John Ruth.

Not only is Norton Judy's all-time favorite Tiger Mountain wine, she's been known to sell it to impossible buyers, like a teetotaler with a "Jesus Saves" bumper sticker and a beer-guzzling motorcyclist with tattoos and leather boots.

13

Departing Dog Days for *La Fête des Vignerons*

It is the dog days of August in Georgia when we board Air France to see what we can learn from the small family vineyards in southern France. The heat index in Tiger was 100 degrees when we left—the temperatures are in the mid-90s in Atlanta as well, with the thick, humid air hanging like a wet sheet over the steamy landscape.

We had been invited almost a year ago by a Swiss friend to come to the legendary *La Fête des Vignerons*, "festival of the winegrowers," in Vevey, a wine festival that occurs only every twenty-five years. It is based on the ancient custom created by the Brotherhood of Winegrowers (*la Confrerie des Vignerons*) in the seventeenth century to recognize the work of rural grape growers. The growers traditionally brought their harvest to the village to be judged by district wine aficionados. One of the *vignerons* is crowned king of the festival at the opera performance that always depicts (in a unique way for each festival) the seasons of the grape, from bud break to harvest. The opera is composed by renowned European musicians and choreographers.

The historic celebration takes place where it originated—in the magical town of Vevey on Lake Geneva, where the lake and sky melt together on the horizon in delicious blues, the perfect backdrop for lilting white sails on the water and wispy dancing clouds above. We visited Vevey many years ago when it was not nearly the sophisticated resort it is today.

John toils long days for many weeks to get our young vineyards in good enough shape to leave in July for the two-week trip. Arriving late at the farm on those July Friday evenings (having drawn consecutive dates to be "late proofer" of our weekend editorial section), I am up at 6:00 A.M. Saturdays and Sundays helping John tend the vineyards. We are behind in tying our newly planted Viognier vines to poles and training them on the five vertical wires on either side, and we spend days "combing down" the undisciplined Norton canes so that the developing green grape bunches will hang untangled as they ripen.

Deep in our suitcases and carefully encased in bubble wrap are four bottles of our very own Tiger wine to share with our Swiss friends, Silvia Kocher and Peter Ehrensberger, and our French friends, Jean and Marie-Claude Cases, whom we will visit in Laroque des Alberes in southwest France on the first leg of our trip. Silvia is family to us; she lived in our Denver home when our son John was only three years old and I had just entered law school. She speaks French as well as Swiss German; when our girls were eight and nine, they learned from Silvia to love French. They sang with her after dinner each evening and taught their younger brother French nursery rhymes. (All three of our children studied in France during college and speak French.) Silvia later married Peter, who runs Vevey's historic Hotel du Lac where we will stay. My newspaper position only allows two weeks off per year—so I am blowing it all and wondering what I will do when some vineyard crisis or event arises that requires me to be in Tiger longer than a weekend.

Nevertheless, when Silvia alerted us to this incredible fete a year ago and urged us to take her offer of reservations at the hotel, we couldn't refuse. The highlight is the outdoor opera in which the townspeople and many of their animals have roles. It's staged in a huge amphitheater on the lake, one built just for the spectacular performance.

We fly to Paris and then Geneva where we rent a car and drive to Annecy. We will travel first to see the Cases, come back through the vineyards of Bordeaux and the Medoc, and end our trip with the fete in Vevey. Still jet-lagged, we stop at a small inn on Le Lac d'Annecy the first night. On a late afternoon walk, I spot plantain trees leading to an international garden of trees in a city park by the lake. Ever since I wrote my newspaper series about trees, I am constantly looking for unusual textures of bark. The plantain bark is intricately patterned, with irregular gray, beige, and lemon streaks as if an artist had designed each massive trunk, no two alike.

I ask a young woman carrying fresh bread from the bakery how old the trees are. "*Tres vieux, Madam*," she replies. She pauses and adds in broken English, "I love these twisted roots, like croissants with too much—how you say?—rising, yes?" She is delightful; her English is better than my French (although I try to use it a little), and we converse quite well. I learn she is the daughter of the bakery owner. I can hardly wait to stop in the morning for fresh croissants.

Typical of our traveling spontaneity, we seldom make reservations ahead of time, so we head out the next day early, looking always for *Ferme Chambre* signs—bed and breakfast inns or farms where we meet delightful villagers and enjoy local fare.

John calls Coach regularly to check on the vineyard and the weather in Tiger. I snuggle up to John nightly—on lumpy beds and luxurious ones—with a renewed sense of our mutual joy in each other. Fourteen days is the longest we have been together for five years.

After a couple of additional sightseeing jaunts the next day, we head southwest toward the Pyrenees, to the Lanquedoc-Rousillon region. Our friend Jean Cases, like John, has returned to the land of his ancestors. Jean and Marie-Claude welcome us to a perfect patio dinner under a grape arbor and open fine aged wines from Jean's cellar. Our oldest daughter, Shelly, lived with the Cases on a summer high school exchange program; Agnes Cases and Shelly are friends who still stay in touch.

The next morning John and I climb Mount Canigou with Jean. The mountain is a spiritual symbol for the Catalan people, and a thirteenth-century abbey is still operating near its peak.

"See, Marta," Jean says with his thick accent, "here is the circle of ancient stones. Fire was invented in this place."

"I suppose by a Catalan man," I reply with a laugh. "Exactly, *c'est vraie* [it's true]," he responds in a serious tone.

He reminds us always that he is a Catalan man, with Roman roots, and he takes us to all of the historic Catalan sites in his hometown of Laroque. A financier, he has lived all over the world. But now, Jean has retired and taken up painting, focusing also on his wine collection, his garden, and his family. He and Marie-Claude take us to dinner one evening in nearby Perpignan where there is a Catalan dance in the city plaza.

John and I try to be good sports and join the dancing, but the intricate tapping steps, which look so easy, are incredibly complicated. Jean tells us that the Catalan used the dances during World War II to tap messages to the French Resistance with whom they sympathized.

Laroque is tucked between the mountains, the sea, and the border with Spain. There is much to see all around: we visit the fishing village and harbor at Collioure and the small café where Matisse, Picasso, and so many other famous French artists spent time. We go also to Boulou in the Lanquedoc to see the cork trees. Jean comments on the dreadful plastic corks he hears are becoming vogue in America. "Never at Tiger Mountain," John declares.

We visit Marie-Claude's brother who owns vineyards, and we learn his grapes are Grenache, Syrah, Mourvedre, and Merlot, also Cot—which we are especially excited about. Cot grapes are what we know as Malbec.

John speaks no French and Marie-Claude's brother speaks no English, but he and John are in the vineyards gesturing and shaking their heads excitedly as they examine a leaf disease problem and admire healthy grape clusters not yet ready for harvest.

The day before we leave, Jean takes us to his arboretum, another of his new projects, and we enjoy a picnic on our tour of his many unusual trees.

"Why do you plant trees, Jean?" I ask.

"Why?" he answers with a grin. "I plant trees that will live on because I am afraid to die."

Trees for Jean and vines for John—in the land of their fathers. Perhaps their legacies will live forever. We leave for Bordeaux with many tips from Jean, the wine collector, about the vineyards in St. Emilion, St. Estephe, and the Pomerol that we should visit, as well as where to find Chateau d'Yquem.

Outside of Tiger Mountain, I proclaim St. Emilion, with its ancient cobblestone walks and vineyards around the city, my favorite place on earth. We take the last available room in Au Logis des Ramparts, a small inn on rue Gaudet in the old part of the medieval town. The lace curtains flutter in the open windows, and the sun plays on pale yellow pillows in the ornate chairs. We immediately push the twin beds, decked in frilly white coverlets, together, laughing as we spread out on the bed to pore over a brochure of local restaurants. Two or three are particularly appealing, so we ask the innkeeper, who speaks perfect English, for advice. We decide on Le Clos du Roy. He makes reservations for us at 8:00 P.M., and we have a glass of the hotel's house wine and some cheeses in the courtyard while watching the sunset. Later that evening, we enjoy a delightful dinner—the dessert, a hazelnut parfait with a local Muscat dessert wine, is memorable.

The next day we are off to visit the vineyards. We stop at several small wineries and then arrive at Château Beau-Séjours Bécot, a Premier Grand Cru (the top classification in Bordeaux wines), in the late afternoon, only to realize we should have called for tour reservations. Nevertheless, a young woman greets us at the door and says she is expecting us. (Luckily, we seem to have been mistaken for no-show visitors with reservations, but we say not a word.) She waves us on towards a group of eight who are going to visit the underground cave with a member of the staff. The chateau was once a twelfth-century monastery with a rock quarry beneath the building. It now serves as the family cellar. Were it not so elegant in tiles and candles I might have felt I was going on a Halloween jaunt. The first room displays skulls that were found in the excavation of the monastery. Pointing to hundreds of bottles of wine carefully stored in the cave and meticulously labeled, our guide says, "This is the family 'bank.'" On our way out, we stop to admire the barrel room, lit by giant chandeliers, with barrels showing perfect, pink stripes between the center staves washed or painted with the "lees" of the wine, the particles that precipitated to the bottom of the barrel during fermentation. Our red wine barrels have wine stains in uneven splotches around the bungholes, and I ask John why we can't mimic these artful barrels. (The bunghole is the opening through which the wine is drained. It has a cork-like cap or "bung.") But John is fascinated instead with the wood wedges that provide an interesting stacking pattern for the barrels.

"We could do that," he whispers to me. "It would save buying so many barrel racks."

The highlight of our visit, however, is an art show in the grand ballroom of the chateau. The abstract paintings on black background with vivid designs, by Michael Pourteyron, are displayed inside lighted stainless steel tanks that normally hold wine.

Guests sip wine and peer in the lighted tanks in a grand ambiance. Judging from the prices on the art, Pourteyron is well known, and we buy a signed poster on our way out.

The next day, we stop in some of the vineyards in the Pomerol, one of the smallest and most fascinating regions in Bordeaux. John hops out of the car when he spots a man dropping clusters of grapes in his Cabernet Franc vineyard. Beautiful clusters, not quite ready for harvest, lie all over the vineyards; the vineyard owner tells John that he must thin to only two clusters per cordon.

"Does that mean we should be dropping more fruit?" I ask John afterward.

"The limitation on the number of clusters per vine may be a requirement of the appellation—the St. Emilion area's own regulations for wine growers," he says, "but I've always heard the Pomerol doesn't abide by those regulations and still produces exceptional wines." He adds that we have a different trellis system and such different growing conditions that he's not sure, and I can tell he intends to find out.

We visit wineries with incredibly beautiful barrel rooms, but one of my favorite places is a local cooperative at St. Estephe where twenty-three growers bring their grapes to be crushed, fermented, and aged—in cement vats in the walls. We learn, though, that some of the better quality grapes go into metal tanks and barrels for aging. We buy a couple of bottles for picnicking and discover they are reminiscent of a Beaujolais. The villagers drink the local wines at lunch and dinner, and with great enjoyment.

"*Le vin est la vie, n'est pas?* [Wine is life, right?]" says an old man who walks slowly past our picnic under a shade tree. We offer him a glass of wine, but he refuses and wanders on.

John puts our rolled-up tablecloth down for a pillow and we lie in the grass. He is soon napping. I keep thinking about the contagious joy that permeates the cooperative where the villagers celebrate their fruit, life, and wine—and seem to want no more, just that. It makes me feel guilty about my own failure to enjoy each day in our vineyards, the daily doing of it, the beauty of each season, instead worrying about how it will all turn out for the future.

Wishing we had time to explore the nearby Cahors region where our French-style Malbec originates, we head instead toward Lake Geneva. The lakeside town of Vevey greets us with festive banners lining its narrow streets. The Hotel du Lac, normally restrained and understated, is bustling with young people. Silvia seems her same happy self, despite working as a hostess and juggling events. The first thing she asks of John is that he play "Danny Boy" on the piano in the hotel lobby. We share memories with Silvia of her stay in our home. After a long day or late surgery, John's "therapy" is to come in and play the piano. "Danny Boy" is one of the pieces in his short "repertoire."

The fete, Silvia explains, is always the story of the seasons of the grape with a different twist each quarter century. Both of her children have roles in the performance and, under the tutelage of costume experts, helped make their own costumes, as is the tradition. In the performance, all in French, the spring buds break to music and dancing. After spring comes summer, then fall harvest with dancers in purple costumes. Stern-looking wine judges, giant marionettes carried by children, arrive amidst the celebration to judge the grapes. A simple grape grower, Arlevin, is the main character in the opera and is crowned king of the festival. He celebrates by drinking too much wine and passes out. The rest of the performance is his dream, from escapades with the red Swiss guard to herding sheep with dyed blue wool and dancing with mermaids that rise from the lake.

The vineyards—young ballet dancers in flowing chartreuse dresses with leafy grape crowns on their heads—are my favorites. They are lined up in perfect "rows" on the vineyard slopes of the stage.

"I think of our Tiger vineyards that way," I tell Silvia, "alive, moving, and changing."

One evening before we leave, John and I are invited to dinner with the Ehrensberger family in the charming 300-year-old house in La-Tour-de-Peilz, a house once owned by a local grape grower. Stunning purple, yellow, and red flowers overflow a balcony that looks out on the lake. Over wine and hors-d'oeuvres, Peter gets out his *Le Nez du Vin* ("The Nose of Wine"), a wonderful leather case containing an array of tiny bottles that give off the aromas or "nose" of different wines—

chocolate, leather, rose petal, pepper, blackberry, vanilla, cinnamon, and others. There is one set for reds and another for whites. It's fun to pass them around and guess what the scent is, a great wine tasting exercise since the aromas of wine are more than half the sensory experience.

We are curious where can we purchase such a thing, which would be a perfect gift for our connoisseur son-in-law. Peter makes a phone call; then, he and John hop on a couple of the bikes at the house—no driving the village streets during the Fête—and return with the gift, purchased just minutes before the store closed for the evening. After salad and raclette, so traditionally Swiss, we enjoy more wine and serious conversation. Peter, ten years older than Silvia, tells us that as he ages, he wants to leave behind something permanent. For a couple of decades now, he has worked to put Hotel du Lac on the map as a top resort. He has little time for his favorite things, fishing and sailing, although he has his own boat and does both periodically.

"To do something you love very well is satisfying enough," I say, sensing his pride in his hotel's reputation.

"No—," he replies, "it is *not* sufficient." Silvia says she enjoys her family and hotel position, overseeing the finances, as well as writing for a parenting magazine.

"I don't feel the need to leave a great legacy," she adds.

John says for him the most important thing is to leave educated and happy children who are prepared to contribute to society. Silvia agrees. John takes pride in his surgery, but says it is the interaction with people that gives him reward, whether patients or family. Peter says he's still searching and that even a fine family isn't all of it. I agree with Peter about the lifelong search for meaning and promise to leave a book some day as a part of my own legacy.

We return for our last evening at the hotel. A gentle rain falls, and we leave the balcony doors open to the lake, while a soft breeze and the muted sounds of partygoers in the streets lull us to sleep. The next morning as we enjoy cheeses, jams, and fresh croissants on the hotel patio, I'm thinking of what we have back home to match a French breakfast when Silvia's daughter comes to visit in a few years. The breads we can't begin to match, so maybe something very American, like Krispy Kreme donuts in the city and blueberry pancakes at the farm.

As our plane lifts off from Geneva into a crisp, sun-streaked sky, all I can think of is the old song based on a Rod McKuen poem that I used to listen to in college when John and I were dating, "I'll catch the sun and never give it back again. I'll catch the sun and keep it for my own."[11]

Back to my own frantic life—a happy frantic—in Atlanta and Tiger.

---

[11] Rod McKuen, "I'll Catch the Sun," lyrics from *Caught in the Quiet* (London/New York: Montcalm Productions, Inc., 1970).

14

A Gold Medal, CNN, and the *San Francisco Chronicle*

Owners of a bed and breakfast in Clayton, Gayle and David Darugh, suggest we enter our Cabernet Franc in the American Wine Society competition. Dave serves as legal counsel to the national organization. The Darughs' Beechwood Inn, a historic log house in Clayton, is already attracting wine lovers and gourmands, and both Gayle and David are wine connoisseurs and gourmet cooks.

We hesitate.

Dave explains that we have nothing to lose. It's a blind tasting (so no Georgia wine prejudice) with well-qualified judges, and if we don't win anything, no one even knows we entered.

Later that month, the Darughs call us excitedly from the American Wine Society's national meeting. Our Cabernet Franc has won a gold medal in a crowded class of red *vinifera* varietals. We are stunned.

I attend an AWS reception and tasting held in Atlanta a few weeks later for the winning wineries. (John is called to perform emergency surgery—nothing new in our lives—and can't come with me as planned.) When I arrive, I note the predominant number of California tables. Our table is near the back of the reception area but graced with a vase of lovely blue hydrangeas.

When the first guests arrive, a gentleman dressed in a dapper tweed jacket and bow tie with small spectacles perched on his nose comes to our table. "Would you like to taste our Tiger Mountain Cabernet Franc?" I ask. "Where *is* Tiger Mountain?" he inquires. I tell him we're located in the Blue Ridge Mountains of North Georgia, and he visibly recoils, pulling his glass back. "No, no thank you…I don't think so," he says and heads to a table of Napa Valley wines nearby with slick, sexy ice wine bottles all around. John and I chuckle afterwards about the California wine snob factor, but it's a story I keep in mind, a reminder of the obstacles a Georgia winery must overcome.

A few weeks later, I attend a wine tasting in a suburban Atlanta wine shop to hear *Wall Street Journal* wine columnists John Brecher and Dorothy Gaiter. They are friends of my *Journal-Constitution* editor, so I introduce myself as a fellow journalist and local winery owner, and I manage to get two bottles of our wines in their hands afterward.

Brecher and Gaiter are, I know, true believers in promoting local wines wherever they go—consistent with their theory that almost every state in the country produces a wine that reflects the unique characteristics of the location, the soils, and even the culture of the region. I love their "un-snobby" approach to helping people with varying degrees of sophistication enjoy a wine experience, a memory, a trip, or a friendship. Every year, they promote a February 28th event joined by thousands around the country and world who read their *Wall Street Journal* column: "Open that Bottle Night." It's based on the notion—and real anecdotes—that folks often hold onto a rare or expensive bottle of wine, saying it will only be better with age, until the special people in their lives they intend to share it with are gone.

Some months after their Atlanta visit, the two wine writers are interviewed on CNN. They take several bottles of wine to Aaron Brown's *NewsNight* show,[12] among them, a bottle of Tiger Mountain Rabun Red. Shelly happens to catch the show from her home in Denver and calls her Dad excitedly—"Dad, our wine is on CNN." It's a Friday evening, and I'm on the road between Atlanta and Tiger.

"Sure, Shelly, our wines are on CNN—what's the joke?" John responds.

"Hurry up, Dad, turn on the TV!" Shelly fairly squeals into the phone as John catches the very end of the segment.

About that time, I arrive, exhausted from the Friday night traffic and fling my week's laundry down as I open the door to John's "Guess what—guess what?!"

I talk to Shelly too, and we all discover that the show will run again after midnight. John and I set our alarm lest we doze off before then so we can see a re-run of Tiger Mountain's CNN debut. Brecher and Gaiter talk about their "Open that Bottle" night, but they also share their penchant for trying local wines wherever they go. They mention several. Then, the camera zooms in on a couple of bottles of wine that they've brought along and—wow—Rabun Red is in great

---

[12] CNN *Newsnight* with Aaron Brown, March 15, 2002.

company! There is a 1982 Barola that they describe, signed by the Italian winemaker, and next to it shines the bottle of Rabun Red with its purple and chartreuse label, our little crooked mountain making a splash on camera.

"This came from Georgia," Gaiter tells *Newsnight* host Brown. "From Georgia as in the old Soviet (Georgia)," Brown replies. "No, no," Gaiter says with a laugh, "as in Atlanta." Then, Breecher chimes in: "We happened to be in Atlanta a couple of weeks ago. We saw this... and last night we thought we would bring it by.... and share it with you," says Gaiter.

Gaiter pours a little into a Styrofoam cup Brown sticks out. "Not bad," he says, swishing around the wine. "Not bad."

"Let's ship him a couple of bottles and tell him to try it in a real glass," I say to John after watching a late night re-run of the show.

Later, we do ship two bottles to Brown at CNN headquarters in New York, but who knows if they made it through security; we never heard back. We obtain a transcript of the interview and share it, of course, with all of our friends. We were already, and know we will always be fans of Brecher's and Gaiter's *Wall Street Journal* wine column.

As spring approaches, more visitors stop at our tasting room, which we keep open only on weekends. The tasting room doubles as a cooled barrel room and has an organic, earthy feel. Thanks to Leckie, we always have a huge vase of fresh flowers on the round tabletop set on three barrels and fine aged cheeses for our guests. At first, we don't even have a cash register, just change in a cigar box. We four take turns selling wine on weekends, but John is sure we could sell during the week, too, so he makes a sign for the tasting room door that says, "If you want to taste our wines, call Judy Ruth or look for John Ezzard in the vineyards." He, of course, adds Judy's home phone. As always, Judy is a good sport, jokingly threatening to charge us for a full time security guard. People love the sign, and it's not long before visitors during the week either call Judy or knock on the door of the rock house. Others drive or walk to the vineyards behind the winery and talk to John, who happily hops off his tractor or stops whatever vineyard work he's doing to sell a few bottles of wine. As Judy says, John has a good sense of priorities.

One day Bill and Leckie suggest we start a wine club. John and I agree it is a good idea. I propose calling it Tigerwine Tasters, which doesn't sound so "clubby" but perhaps will get some attention. We brainstorm ideas for getting more people, especially from Atlanta, to the winery; we've found that visitors to the tasting room love seeing the vineyards, too. We decide to open the club to customers who buy one case of wine up front and pledge to buy another within a year. We will reward them with a 20 percent discount on the first case and on all other wines they buy at the winery as long as their two-case-per-year membership is current. We are thrilled when we get about a dozen couples, all close friends of one or the other of us, to join right off. Taking cues from other wine clubs we've read about, we also decide, as our membership grows, to offer two "invitation only" parties annually to reward our members, a harvest party in the fall and a spring celebration. John suggests that we let club members bring guests, rightly thinking that may bring us more members. He also insists we invite our guests to pick grapes as part of the harvest party. We bounce around ideas for the spring event.

"If we could just get a hundred members by the end of the year," John says.

Bill gets some cards made describing Tigerwine Tasters. We all agree that we need to start our own website. I talk to one of my colleagues at the newspaper, and he offers to design the site in exchange for a case of wine.

Things are moving so fast now that we four are living in a state of stress, but it's what you might call exuberant stress.

Meanwhile, I am acutely aware that the wine business is gobbling up all of our spare time as I race back and forth every weekend from the city to Tiger to help John with the vines, throw dinner parties for various wine lovers (and sometimes wine writers), and return exhausted to my Monday morning editorial duties. Amazingly enough, I am never out of ideas for my column or for the editorials we board members churn out daily, and I am totally absorbed in my world of current events and writing once I am back in the city.

In Tiger, between his part-time medical practice and vineyard and winery demands, John has no time to cultivate the kind of golf and fishing cadre of male friends that were so much a part of his life in Denver. He relishes every season of the grape, though, and even after a long day of surgery, he will head out to the vineyards and work until dark—especially when it's pruning season, his favorite challenge ("where great wines begin," he says). Now, it's almost time for another bud break, and on Fridays when I arrive, he wants me to get in the rusty white truck with him before I even have a chance to change into my jeans and make a "tour" to see how the vines are doing—which ones look as if they may not bud out this time and which look absolutely perfect, with buds swelling and canes "bleeding" as they come alive to the warmth of the April sun. We know by now that we will lose a few vines each year, and spring is the time to order replacements. But it's also a magical time to savor new life and the miracle of a new vintage.

This Friday, as I climb into the truck and kick off my heels from work, I have great news: a top Atlanta gourmet shop, Star Provisions, wants to carry our local wines. The shop is associated with one of Atlanta's five star restaurants, Bacchanalia, whose mantra is local and organic foods. I often stop at Star, not far from my newspaper office downtown, to buy cheeses and fresh baked breads before driving to the farm on Fridays.

A couple of months ago, we finally surmounted the bureaucratic obstacles to final approval of our wholesale license, permissible for small wineries in most states. It allows us to sell directly to commercial outlets instead of going through a distributor. Getting the license is an incredibly cumbersome process. John and I had already found a couple of wine shops in Atlanta interested in our wines, but my big news that the manager of Star Provisions had agreed to carry Tiger Mountain wine is great fun to share. I had given Michael O'Connor, the manager and sommelier, some sample bottles a couple of weeks ago. Even though I'd die to be listed in the restaurant, just getting our wines on the shelf of the small, upscale shop is a coup. Bill had also convinced a popular wine and spirits store near his law office, Pearson's, in Buckhead, to carry some of our wines.

A few weeks later, I go to Star Provisions to shop again and Michael asks me for a couple of extra bottles of Norton to take with him to a course he's taking from Doug Frost, a renowned master sommelier in Kansas City. Not long after that, John receives a call from Frost, who asks to taste some of our other wines. John ships him samples of our first vintages of Cabernet Franc, Touriga Nacional, and Tannat. Later Frost phones again and asks John to ship a couple of bottles to England to a wine writer, Tom Stevenson. John obliges, still not sure of the reason, but flattered that Frost wants to share our wines with someone important in the wine world.

One day, a friend e-mails to say our Touriga and Tannat have received great kudos in the *San Francisco Chronicle.* It's only then that we discover how important Frost is in wine circles. He's the author of several wine books and one of three in the world with both Master Sommelier and Master of Wine credentials. In his July 24, 2003, article in the *Chronicle*, titled "The Wine States of America," he describes "the explosion of high quality wines" in states other than California. He surveys wines in each region of the country, highlighting a few states where the wine industry is making surprising progress. When he gets to the South, he focuses mostly on Virginia and even runs a photo of a bottle of Horton's Norton. Then, under a section titled Southeast, he writes,

> In the rest of America's southeast and to the south of Virginia, most of the wines have been forgettable at best. A dramatic exception is Tiger Mountain Vineyards in Tiger, Ga. Its bottlings of Norton and Cabernet Franc are good; the Tannat ($23) and Touriga Nacional ($25), made from port grape varieties are showstoppers.... How many of these far-flung wines are worth a search. A few. Tiger Mountain's Touriga is one. (Section D-5)

We are ecstatic! I'm ready to roll with the article, ready to put it in every marketing packet.

"But wait," John says. "We've got some new wineries in North Georgia who will be fine competitors before we know it." I agree.

"Maybe we shouldn't use the part about most wines south of Virginia being forgettable," I reply. "Some of the more promising vineyards in North Georgia aren't even producing yet—but I do love the part about one dramatic exception being Tiger Mountain."

"You'll just have to suppress your scrappy nature this once," John preaches to me. "We need to do everything we can to support creation of a critical mass of wineries in North Georgia making fine dry wines."

I waste no time in using excerpts from the Frost article for marketing, quoting the lines about our Touriga and Tannat being "showstoppers" in our latest brochure.

Over a take-out dinner one Friday evening after our usual vineyard tour to check the vines, John and I discuss how to tackle our new commercial market challenge. I had already started putting some materials together for a marketing pack, including our new brochure, quotes from the Frost article, and a price list. But first, John says, we must decide the details of a May "Awakening the Vines" party and the design of an invitation for our wine club members and their guests.

"Yes, and look what I found in the *New York Times* about bud break traditions in eastern Europe," I say. "I've got a great idea."

15

The Seed and Feed Abominables Awaken the Vines

The spring rain persists for the first three days in May. The ground is saturated. The grass on the knoll under the old oak trees squishes under my feet. We are less than a week away from our fourth annual Awakening the Vines celebration, and I am getting nervous about the weather. I think about the previous spring festivals we've staged—most of them on glorious, crisp, blue-sky days.

Our Awakening the Vines party has become a talked-about event, like none other, say our wine club members for whom we stage it.

Many of our most faithful wine buyers come from the Atlanta metro area, almost two hours away, so we wanted to plan a unique event for them. One day, I shared an article with John and our partners that I had found in the *New York Times* about villagers in Croatia who, even during war years, came out to dance and roast sausages in their small vineyards in spring to wake the vines as they had done for centuries. We decided to create our own "Awakening the Vines" festival with live music and dancing in the vines and make it an invitation-only party to reward our wine club members and their special guests. John added the bonfire dimension—the burning of the pruned canes as a symbolic good-bye to winter. For our first awakening party, we hired the local high school brass section. While excellent players, they weren't nearly a big enough sound or a flamboyant enough group for what we had in mind. Shortly after that, we discovered an incredible musical outfit in Atlanta, The Feed and Seed Marching Abominables, and we booked them for our very next spring party.

The musicians—complete with brightly painted horns, drums, crazy costumes, and hats—help make the party the spectacular celebration it has come to be. Some people actually join our wine club just to get an invitation.

The vineyard setting against Tiger Mountain in spring is also spectacular. The vines are chartreuse in early May; delicate pink buds encased in ruffled green, opening up as if from a cocoon to announce a new vintage. The rose bushes at the end of each row of vines seem to shout their vibrant tangerine tones as if competing with all other blooming things that make an Appalachian spring so extraordinary. The huge mound of pruned canes John saves and carefully stacks beyond the barn in front of the oldest of our three vineyards is ready for the annual bonfire and urges partygoers to bid adieu to winter and toast a new vintage.

We know, of course, that much of this spring show in our vineyards is weather sensitive.

And this particular week, the bonfire-to-be has a tarp over it, and John says we'll need a tent on Saturday for our estimated 300 guests. A huge rented tent will cost a cool $1,500 of our wine sale profits, but it's not really profit that motivates us for the Awakening party—it's sharing the excitement of a new season and a taste of our Tiger earth.

Wine, if anything, is an earthy experience. Every year, we add more locally grown dishes and embellish the décor with wild flowers, branches of cherry blossoms and wild azalea, brimming over pottery pitchers on the cheese table, edible flowers sprinkled over tossed salads. There are giant bowls of locally grown strawberries on the dessert table to complement homemade pound cakes—almond, lemon, chocolate—lovingly baked by John's sister, Lucy. They contain enough cream cheese and butter to last me from one spring to the next, but our wine club members have come to rely on them as part of our party. Local, yes—but with farm-to-table elegance.

Most of these festivities can go on in a tent in the rain—we know that, but if it rains, it won't be "the best ever" Awakening party. And as our little farm winery gains momentum, we're in the habit of topping our previous best, be it vintage or party, each time around.

The costumed performance of the Abominables has evolved into an outrageously entertaining show—with players wearing tiger-stripe leotards, sparkling shirts, hats dripping with leaves and grapes, and even wine glasses perched on top. The group has grown larger too—this year I expect almost fifty musicians. They perform no matter what the weather and are mostly professional people—lawyers, doctors, actors, all of whom love to play and dance and let it all hang out. They tote red horns, banners, and painted drums; always there is a Bacchus in the entourage. Anyone who comes to our party in a sour mood can't stay that way long.

They "hide" in the barn and burst forth to the delight of our guests, who clap and laugh at the comical musical show. After the flamboyant opening for hundreds of our picnickers under the old oak trees, the conductor, who often directs the band with a broom, leads the march, with horns blaring, hats bobbing, and banners streaming, past the old red barn to the vineyards where John lights the bonfire near the Tannat vines. The crowd claps in rhythm and follows in a snake-like line to the bonfire. As the flames leap, trumpets play and drummers drum as if it were their last hurrah. They play marches and rumbas and the crowd-pleasing "Hold that Tiger."

My favorite Abominable is Josie Starnes, the mother of an Atlanta city councilwoman I've admired from my newspaper post for her hard work on homelessness in the city. Elegant in her purple feathers, lace shawl, and grape-laden hat from which alluring silver curls peek, Josie always carries a Victorian era pocketbook and often wears ruffled gloves to complement it. She inevitably stops to give me a hug; one year I gave her a lace pocketbook with faux jewels that my daughter, Lisa, found at a vintage shop in California. She loves it. The younger band members play instruments and some dance furiously, but Josie just sways gracefully among the vines. I admire her style.

This soggy week, I'm feeling truly anxious about our Awakening Party. Visions of glorious spring fests past are starting to fade with every thunderclap, and I envision swirls of smoke instead of bright flames from our damp stack of winter canes. For the first time, we are facing a spring festival in what could be driving rain and wind—not just "scattered showers" are forecast but torrents of rain.

No-ooo, please no-ooo, I moan, having printed out the weekend forecast for my husband from the Weather Channel website.

"Shall we call a rain date?" I ask.

"For 300 people?" John replies. "Don't be silly—the party goes on."

I change the voicemail message at the winery to assure callers the party is on, rain or shine. "Wine, artisan cheeses, and a gourmet lunch under the big tent," I say in my cheeriest voice, "don't miss the Abominables, who will dance in the vineyards to wake the buds."

John starts calling tent rental companies nearby, and I wonder what we will do with buckets of leftover pasta and stacks of sausages. Bad weather can cause a lot of no-shows, especially for club members coming from Atlanta or other places that require a long drive. Some stay over in nearby lodges and B&Bs, creating a nice tourism boost for our mountain community.

So far, reservations are still pouring in. It's pouring outside too—three days before our spring bash. I try to ignore the pitter-patter on our metal roof, a sound I normally adore. I must focus on the last-minute details of party planning for 300, assuming they all show up. Where is my checklist? Let's see—give a reminder call to my friend Cindy Halbkat, who makes wonderful organic pasta salads each spring for us and delivers them in huge white buckets; this year I've asked for a Thai peanut dressing and the addition of fava beans to the sun dried tomatoes, fresh veggies, and bow tie pasta. I stop to place my favorite large pottery salad bowls out in the kitchen, ready to be hauled with other serving dishes and cheese boards to the tables under the old oak trees. The bright gingham cloths, freshly pressed, and thirty small, blooming plants (shhh—from Walmart!), one for each picnic table, are ready to go.

Now I'll organize the cheese boards and knives. The rounds of aged cheeses I've ordered from two Georgia dairies in South Georgia, Sweet Grass in Thomasville and Flat Creek in Swainsboro, will arrive shipped in cold packs tomorrow. My downstairs refrigerator is running over with various kinds of "healthy" sausages: sun dried tomato, artichoke, smoked chicken and apple, and a few chorizo for those who like spicy. Our assistant winemaker, Jabe Hilson, is a terrific griller and has a whole team of young friends who love grilling at our parties. Our new tasting room manager, Jon Engel, has turned out to be excellent party planning help. Still, some of the details are only in my head.

Mustard? Do we have brown and Dijon as well as honey mustard? Who was supposed to buy the condiments for the sausages? I get the bright dishes out for them that we bought in Sonoma, orange, yellow, and chartreuse, and the small knives with colored handles that by luck match them—the knives, a special gift from my neighbor on Tiger Mountain, Judy Freedland, who entertains with impeccable taste. "They just looked like you and the winery," she said when she gave them to me, not for a birthday or a holiday gift, but for fun, because she couldn't wait for me to have them.

Let's see, Judy Ruth ordered six hundred purple napkins and chartreuse paper plates ages ago, but what about small paper plates for the cheese table—and what about serving dishes and cake stands for the dessert table? Jabe will buy ten gallons of freshly picked local strawberries from Osage, the fruit and vegetable market up the road where berries are picked every morning from the field behind the market; we'll put them in the two giant glass bowls I bought last year for them. We always try to support other local farms. (At the fall harvest party we serve tomato mozzarella because we can count on late-season local tomatoes and fresh basil from the same market in September.) Wait—who did we assign to wash all of those strawberries? Jon knows, I hope. Maybe somebody better call and see what the rain will do to the strawberry picking schedule. We may have to pick up the berries on Thursday; it's forecast to be the only dry day this week.

What is that upstairs noise? It's hail on our metal roof—what if it does that Saturday? Once, hail damaged our tiny grapes, bruising them, and making some turn hard. But it's too early for that type damage this time. I hope hail won't hurt the delicate buds at this stage. John doesn't seem worried. He's calling the mowers to make sure they come Thursday, even if the grass is wet, before the tent goes up.

I leave my party checklist momentarily to admire the tiny nuthatches at my birdfeeder—they always scoot down the tree trunk to the feeder, black and white heads bobbing. Everything is lush green and the roses are perfect, their tiny tangerine buds just beginning to open. But if it's stormy, who will even see them? Our bonfire could be a smoldering mess.

I make a quick call to the Abominables—dancing in the rain is not a problem; it will be fun, "splashy," says the director. On a similarly cheerful note, Judy, our faithful winery administrator, calls to say two more wine club members are bringing eight guests each. What have I forgotten? And when will we ever have a special events coordinator so party details aren't so precariously stored in my head? And when will we make enough profit to build a kitchen at the winery so we don't have to haul all the serving dishes and cheese boards from our house? Shelly says it wouldn't matter—I'd still want my big, colorful pottery bowls on the round wooden tabletops that sit fittingly on three wine barrels each. She's right—Appalachian pottery is part of the party's authentic character.

What else have I forgotten? I have forgotten to confirm the salad greens order—that's what. Probably fifteen pounds of greens will be enough though I tentatively ordered twenty, organic, with lots of arugula. The dried cranberries can be picked up at the same time from Grapes and Beans in town, and we have red onions on hand. I give up on who can slice them—I'll just do it myself this year. Cindy will once again bring edible flowers to decorate the green salad and her special citrus dressing, a better complement for wine than any vinegar-type dressing. My walking pals, the three women I walk three miles with every morning, are my reliable salad servers. They belong to the wine club and will always work, they say in their familiar laughing voices, for wine.

That reminds me that we never have plastic containers to

give away some of the leftover food to our volunteer workers. Maybe Jabe can get those.

Check off cheeses—or did I do that already?—they're arriving by UPS overnight tomorrow. Identifying the cheeses on my ceramic cheese markers (with washable black pen, of course) is one of my special joys: Greenhill Brie, Low Country Gouda, Cypress Cheddar, Thomasville Tomme, Pecan Chevre, and this year, an Aztec cheese, with beautiful zigzag colors. Who knows if Aztec will be too spicy with wine; I've never ordered it before. And there must be a beautiful pottery dish for my favorite peach mango chutney to go with the brie—chutney made by local organic farmer and writer Joe Gatins.

Check off pound cakes—Lucy has made sixteen of those. She takes care of running off hundreds of nametags, too, with a tiger stripe border. Check off bread. Our dear Atlanta friends, the McMullans, soon to be our new winery partners, will pick up the sixteen loaves I ordered from Buckhead Bread Company—multigrain, walnut raisin, chocolate (great with cheddar), rustic wheat, jalapeno cheddar, and some long baguettes and pretzel bread for show. Eight more loaves, including walnut wheat and rosemary olive, are coming from Annie's Naturally Bakery, just over the state line in Sylva, North Carolina. (Annie's also sells our wines.) The loaves will be sliced at the bakery, but our volunteer bread crew will cut them into smaller pieces for the cheese baskets. I have a wonderful new "old" Doughboy to pile the interesting bread in alongside the huge cheese boards John's cousin made with the Tiger Mountain logo on them. Our loyal friends, high school classmates of John's, the Easterlins, will bring a huge Vidalia onion dip and Anne McMullan, the McMullans' daughter who attended culinary school, will send the best paté in the world, complete with toast points.

"Don't worry," says John, giving me a needed back massage as we climb in bed. "It will all come together."

"Wine and dirt are naturals," I reply. "Maybe wine and mud will work too."

I sleep fitfully, and Saturday dawns with hanging, dark clouds, but no rain. Despite our weather worries, hundreds arrive, quickly filling the parking lot across the road. The bus carrying the Abominables comes right on time although the driver, trying to avoid the huge mud puddles, hits a few bushes alongside the road to the barn. The musical group is in its usual festive mode. Wine, Tiger Mountain logo glasses, and cheese trays have been placed in the barn for them—on the side of the barn I've redone, with hay on the floor, a coat of fresh paint, country décor on the red board walls, a few rocking chairs, barrels and tables with checkered cloths. We want to pamper the Abominables—they *are* the party.

Wine flows, and the Abominables perform for the crowd, then head toward the vineyards as the crowd claps and lines up behind them. But just as John and friends remove the tarp from the pile of grapevine canes to start the bonfire, there's a cloudburst. Plumes of grey smoke instead of flames rise from the stacked canes, and everyone races back to the tent, laughing and dripping wet. The Abominables play on. Fortunately, there is no lightening, but there are sheets of rain. As the eating and drinking progress in what seems a cozy tent, the grass underneath becomes slick and muddy.

"Have we got any mulch at the house?" John asks frantically. I motion to two workers to follow me in the farm truck and we pick up several big bags of wood chips to spread in the muddiest places under the tent. The Abominables mingle with the crowd, enjoying the food and conviviality. When it's time for them to leave, John cautions the bus driver not to go too far out in the hayfield to turn around, but that's exactly where he heads. Before we know it, the bus is stuck in the mud. The players wave and sing as the wheels spin, spewing hay, gravel and mud.

John is wet from head to toe but valiantly climbs on the tractor with a heavy chain to try to pull the bus out; meanwhile, two men, both guests, bring wide boards and four shovels from the barn. Amidst the mud, pouring rain, and conflicting instructions, the bus driver actually guides the bus out (six tries and a few ditches in the hayfield later). As we bid our revelers good-bye, the tent begins to leak and a pole falls.

In a near state of collapse that evening, I pick at a bowl of leftover pasta John hands me with a glass of Viognier. "I never want to see that pasta again," I respond. "I never want to mastermind another party like this." I'm sobbing.

"Yeah, we have enough sausages left to feed an army," John mutters.

But the next day, phone calls and e-mails tell us everyone had a grand time—"cozy," "memorable," " a barrel of fun," "colorful," " superb local cheeses," "send Lucy's pound cake recipe," and "craziest wine party ever."

Yep—it was that all right.

16

Peddling Wine from an SUV

Nearly a dozen new vineyards are popping up in the North Georgia mountains, and people are getting the idea that Georgia wines are about more than muscadine or—good grief—moonshine! (Moonshine days are never over in Georgia; according to the front page of the *Clayton Tribune*, a still was busted recently in a wooded area north of town.)

With our *San Francisco Chronicle* accolades and a string of medals in hand, John and I decide it's time to launch a commercial market. We have our own wholesale license, permitted for in-state farm wineries in Georgia. Sue Willis, owner of Grapes and Beans, a popular lunch spot in Clayton that also sells fine wines, is excited to add our local wine to her selections.

Next, John and I plan a trip south, to Macon and Savannah where we can also visit friends. The late fall weather makes us feel better about stacking twenty-two cases of wine in the back of our SUV. I make up some marketing packets, nothing more than a card with a listing of our awards, some press clips including the *San Francisco Chronicle* article by Doug Frost, our new rack card, and a colorful label sheet describing each of our wines with a blurb about suggested food pairings.

I decide a large white envelope with one of our labels slapped on the front will do for now to hold the "brag sheets" and the retail/wholesale price list that I run off on some of our logo stationery.

Our first stop is the Oakwood Package Store, an hour from home, just south of Gainesville, where John has already made friends with the local manager, Rusty. I can tell John has that one wrapped up and I'm not needed. Three hours later, we arrive in Macon where we're scheduled to pour wine at the historic Hay House. I am needed here. I whip out some notes I wrote for a workshop we sometimes present, "Wine by the Class." We give a little wine chat to a group of fifty and pour free wine to benefit the local historical society. The contacts we make are well worth it. We enjoy dinner and an overnight with our friends, Patricia and Tom Bass. Both are lawyers, and Tom is chairman of the board of Wesleyan College, where my mother and her two sisters graduated. Back then, it was the preferred women's college for young (white) ladies growing up in South Georgia. It is still a small liberal arts college for women and the oldest women's college in the country. I am encouraged to see the large number of accomplished black students at the school today.

As we drive by the campus, with its huge magnolia trees and stately buildings, I wonder what my mother's and aunts' reaction would be to my peddling wine near their alma mater, previously run by the Methodist Church.

A recent visitor to our winery was from Macon, and she gave John and me a list of four retail wine shops to call on. We hit a home run with the first two, selling each a couple of cases of wine. We are excited about our initial sales in this sleepy middle Georgia town. One wine shop is located near a country club and the other in an attractive shopping center.

The third is in a mixed urban area of town. It's The Depot on Pio Nono Avenue. As we drive up to the huge warehouse-like building with wine and beer signs on it, I see a few homeless people sifting through nearby trashcans. I ask John if he's sure he wants to go in—because it looks like a beer and spirits place. John has already gotten our new shoulder bag wine carrier with the tasting wines in it out of the car; it's obvious he is going to give The Depot the old college try.

Once inside, we ask for the wine buyer, whom John had phoned earlier, and are greeted by Dan Suh, a friendly Korean man, who ushers us to his small dimly lit office. Suh pulls some Reidel glasses off the shelf for tasting, a good sign indeed. He gets out a yellow pad and a dump bucket, and we go through six wines as he takes copious notes. After a while, thinking we will be lucky to sell one case of our wine here, I say in my cheeriest voice, "Oh, by the way, we do sell mixed cases if you want to try a few bottles of more than one wine." He smiles as we pour the last of the reds we've brought, Tannat. "Very interesting," he says, swirling the wine in his glass. "A scent of toasted caramel, I think, and nice tannins." We nod. No one has ever said our Tannat has a touch of toasted caramel, but I take another sip and I decide Suh is right; I've just never been able to identify that flavor which I might only have thought of with a dessert wine, not a full bodied dry one like Tannat.

After a while, Suh tears a sheet off his yellow pad and

hands it to John.

"I see. Very good—you want fourteen bottles," John says.

"No," Suh replies with a hearty laugh. "I want fourteen *cases*." We try hard to contain ourselves, to act as if fourteen cases is an everyday order. But we have never sold that much wine in a single place before.

We are embarrassed that we don't have a full case of everything Suh wants, but we are able to supply nine cases of his chosen varietals, and we promise to have our "driver" (not knowing which cousin or vineyard helper that may be) deliver the other five cases the following week. While John and a store employee are unloading the wine, I peruse the shelves and see that while Suh has a lot of beer and spirits up front, sections behind are devoted entirely to wines, many of them rare and expensive. I spot Opus One, Ferrari Carrano, Cakebread, Dominus, Jordan and Shafer in his California sections, and impressive French wines in the section beyond: Haute Brion, Chateau Mouton Rothchild, and John's favorite, Chateau Margeaux.

I decide spontaneously to buy an expensive bottle of Fonseca port from Suh. John looks irritated with me for doing so, wondering how we're going to keep it cool on our road trip to Savannah.

Suh thanks us, says he is delighted to find a fine Georgia wine and notes that the only local wines he's seen before were sweet wines, mostly muscadine.

It's almost 3 P.M. when we pull away from the Depot and we are both starving. We celebrate with a Big Mac and some fries—why not? We've no time to find a nice restaurant if we keep to our schedule to hit a couple of other market possibilities en route to Savannah. Fast food isn't something I indulge in very often. I pick up the three *Wine Spectator* magazines in the back seat that I have yet to read, thinking Rabun Red might be fine with a Big Mac.

"Maybe we should pour a bottle Rabun Red over our heads," I say to John, still marveling over our big sale.

"Save that thought for the shower tonight," he replies gleefully.

We're running late and have dinner reservations in Savannah at Gottlieb's, a restaurant that would be perfect for our wines—and the sommelier is expecting us. First we want to stop in the small town of Dublin at a wine shop recommended to us by a friend. The owner, who told us on the phone this morning that he'd be there, isn't, so we leave some sample bottles and hit the road for Savannah once more. John decides to take a "short cut" he knows toward the Georgia coast. Well, a short cut he *once* knew. We get lost, call, and postpone our dinner reservation by an hour, and finally wind our way along the back roads of Lowndes County toward Savannah. It's dusk and we are on a two-lane road. Suddenly, we see a flashing blue light coming toward us. (Lowndes County is renowned in Georgia for speed enforcement.) A sheriff's deputy meanders to the window. I can hardly wait to see what John is going to say; he nearly always weasels his way out of tickets, and I seem never to be able to do so. Maybe with small town cops, it's a guy thing. If anyone can turn on the Southern charm, John can.

"I'm sorry officer," he says immediately, " I know, I

know—I forgot to dim my lights for the oncoming car, and I might have had a bit of a heavy foot on the pedal."

The officer, who has a great Southern drawl, spits his tobacco and chuckles. "Thass right, thass exactly what you did wrong," he says, looking at John's license. "Hmm, Tiger, Georgia."

"We've got a family farm up there in the mountains," John says.

The officer nods and chuckles. "I'll tell you what. I'm jest gonna give you a warning this time—but you slow down, doctah."

I'm on the verge of giggles, but instead I fume as we pull away. "What in the world," John says, "are you mad because I *didn't* get a ticket?"

"No—I'm just irritated knowing in the same situation, same officer, I *would* have gotten one."

Now, of course, John's afraid to fudge on the speed limit, and I fear we're going to be late even for our delayed dinner reservation in Savannah. Not the best start for selling our wine to a top restaurant. I decide the country road we're on, nearly devoid of traffic, lends itself to a clothes change in the car. While I brought along a skirt for dinner, after moving a couple of cases of wine in the back seat in order to get to my hanging bag I settle for wiggling into a silk shell and some dressier shoes and jewelry to go with the black capris I'm wearing. I don't exactly feel fresh and beautiful for the sommelier we want to impress; presentable will have to do. All John has to do, of course, is grab his jacket.

The glamour of being small winery owners never ends.

17

Wine Fit for a Five-Star

Our statewide wine marketing trips continue when we can make our individual work schedules jibe. I argue that we need to be listed in key metro restaurants, but John vows to tout our wine to every nook and cranny of Georgia, be it Sleepy's Package Store in Tennille or Grits Café in Forsyth. Admittedly, they are both colorful establishments.

At a wine pouring for a historical society benefit in the middle Georgia town of Sandersville, we learn that the area's wine lovers buy their wines at Sleepy's General Store in the nearby town of Tennille. The manager of the small store is absolutely thrilled to add a fine Georgia wine and also takes one of the wood display racks emblazoned with our logo that we recently commissioned a carpenter friend to make. We give them to retail shops that buy our wines.

Several friends later ask why in the world we want our wines in Tennille—and where in the world is it? Our answer is simple: kaolin.

Georgia is one of a handful of sources in the country for the rare kaolin mineral, which is used in hundreds of products including paints and paper. The Sandersville-based operation is a multi-million-dollar business, and company executives, managers, and employees who live in the area make for a critical mass of wine drinkers in this unlikely part of the state.

The second time Sleepy's orders from us, the owner, who is visiting friends in the area, comes by the winery and picks up the wine himself.

Closer to home, in Gainesville, we meet the owner of The Wagon Wheel, a package store near a popular country club. When Woody Justus finds out John grew up in Rabun County, he smiles broadly. "So did half of my family," he says, and he and John proceed to name all of their cousins and mutual friends. Without tasting a drop of our wine, he orders five cases and a display rack to put them on.

"Wine is like politics," I say to our son on the phone. "It's not a matter of merit or quality but whether folks like you."

"Yeah, but they'll re-order only if the wines sell and the word gets out that Georgia can produce some fine wines," he replies. "But then, by the time you consider the cost of gas and even lodging to haul your wines a long way, you could be playing a losing game." Unfortunately, John Jr., our MBA son, is always giving us the stark cost analysis, often a downer.

"You could be right," I respond glumly.

"Don't worry, Mom," he says, sensing my despair. "You and Dad are doing a great job of establishing your branding across the state."

"It's a real dilemma," I say to John after the conversation with our son. "How in the world are we going to supply these shops and restaurants five and six hours' drive away?"

John shrugs and grins, "Cousins and college kids."

We plan a longer trip to Savannah after harvest, to market our wine and to visit our best friends from Colorado, Don and Karen Ringsby, who have bought an historic three-story house near Forsyth Park, one of the most famous and gorgeous public spaces in the country. Don, one of Denver's outstanding businessmen, is already getting a kick out of asking (in a loud voice) when he goes to a nearby package store if there is any Tiger Mountain Vineyards wine on the shelf. We sell to a bustling wine shop downtown that also offers tastings (invites us to conduct one) and to a charming new restaurant in the historic district, Noble Fare. While we don't exactly sweep the owners of the city's best-known restaurant, Elizabeth's on 37th, off their feet (they'll taste our sample bottles), we add two more wine shops to our list of retail stores in the coastal area.

At the annual High Museum Wine Auction, I make friends with Jerry Klaskala, the chef-owner of one of Atlanta's best restaurants, Aria. He subsequently orders a case of Cabernet Franc and a case of Malbec, which I deliver along with some bonus bottles to Jerry for being an early believer in our little winery. Aria is actually the first top restaurant in the city to list our wines.

Meanwhile, one of my newspaper colleagues suggests that Chantelle Pabros, the sommelier at The Dining Room at the Buckhead Ritz Carlton, might be interested in a local wine. Pabros is one of the youngest sommeliers in the country to head a wine program at a five-star restaurant. I call, but she is in France. I leave a message. A month later, I summon the courage to call her again—only to reach her voice mail once more. Two months go by—and then, out of the blue, she calls to ask if John and I would like to come to dinner on a weeknight at The Dining Room when she can spend some time with us. She asks us to bring some wines for her to taste. We agree on a date, and I make a reservation for the following Wednesday evening.

It's harder and harder to drag John away from the vineyards for any reason. He jealously guards Tuesdays, Wednesdays, and Fridays when he wants to be working in his vines every moment because he is still seeing patients on Mondays and Thursdays. Getting our wines listed in a five-star establishment is just enough to get him out of his jeans briefly—though he likes to make more than one stop during our visits to the city since our marketing and shopping lists grow long. He suggests I make appointments to stop at two or three Whole Foods Stores along the way. One of those is the Alpharetta store in the suburbs. John and the wine buyer, Don Reddicks, have hit it off ever since Reddicks became the first of the Whole Foods buyers to purchase our wine. Now he has a whole section for local wines from Georgia and North Carolina.

"Let's stop and say hello to Don," John says.

That's the difference in our marketing approaches. John is still using the Tiger technique—drop by and be friendly. I prefer to make a specific appointment and try to close a sale all at once. At any rate, I'm able to get in touch with the wine buyers at two other Whole Foods, so we pack the car with sample bottles, including a cooler of ice packs.

I learned the hard way about putting wine in a cooler of loose ice. I did that once on a hot summer day when I was determined to take some wine after work to the sommelier at Bones, one of Atlanta's renowned restaurants. By the time I arrived at the Buckhead restaurant, the labels were soaking wet and rumpled, and the Viognier label had come off altogether. Determined to keep my appointment, I made the incredibly bad call to take the soaking wet bottles in to the sommelier. I can hardly bear to recount the story, but despite expressing sympathy for my summertime direct marketing plight (i.e., out of the car), the sommelier never ordered any wine, and our wines are still not listed at Bones.

John and I strike out for Atlanta in our dinner attire about noon on a hot July day. By the time we have made our three stops, I feel absolutely wilted and wish I had not dressed for dinner when we left. Nevertheless, we arrive in Buckhead for our 6:45 P.M. appointment with the Ritz sommelier. John decides we'll park across the street at Phipps Plaza rather than fool with valet parking at the hotel.

"It's always a wait and we have to drive back to Tiger tonight," he argues when I resist the idea.

As the doorman at the Ritz greets us, I look at my husband aghast. He has left his jacket in the car. "Ties and jackets are required in The Dining Room," I whisper to John. "Everybody knows that. You'd better go back to the car and get your jacket."

"That's ridiculous," John replies as he straightens his tie and looks at his watch, "I'd rather be on time."

"Here, give me the keys. I'll go and get it for you," I respond.

John shakes his head silently.

I know my husband well enough to know my request is hopeless at this point, and that I am just about to cause an unpleasant confrontation before what should be a glorious dinner together.

When we enter the restaurant and are seated, I look around—only to observe that my worst fears are true. There isn't a single man in the restaurant without a jacket.

I fume in silence as the candle flickers on our table against a small vase containing a fresh blue hydrangea and a lovely woman brings us menus and a wine list.

She smiles. "Chantelle is expecting you," she says.

I smile and nod, but I am certain John has blown our singular opportunity to get our Tiger Mountain wine listed in a five-star restaurant, one of Atlanta's longest standing and best known.

Soon the young Chantelle approaches. She is stunningly beautiful with silky dark hair and china-perfect skin. She wears a simple, elegant black dress and neither needs nor wears any jewelry—and she has a smile that would make a Scotch-on-the-rocks guy morph into a fine wine drinker instantly. She acts as if she has known John and me for a long time. She and John immediately strike up a conversation about the unusual grapes we are growing at Tiger, especially the Touriga Nacional, which she quizzes John about in detail. Among other things, she wants to come up and see and touch real vines in a real vineyard; she says she's lost in pourings and dinners and wines in the bottle. She needs to absorb their canes and canopies and growing—unto her soul, it seems.

For appetizers, John orders escargot and I order *foie gras de canard*. A dry German Riesling is delightful with both, but Chantelle suggests that should we ever want to go all out, to announce to guests a great feast in store, we should try pairing a Sauterne with the escargot. I gulp—the only Sauterne we have ever served (only once or twice at a small dinner) is Chateau d'Yquem, which is incredibly expensive. But what's a sommelier for but pairing advice?

For our salad course, Chantelle opens and shares with others in the dining room our Tiger Mountain Petit Manseng, which is favorably received. I'm enjoying baby spinach with goat cheese and walnuts, and John's having hearts of Romaine with mozzarella and basil tomatoes. The tanginess of the Petit Manseng seems just right with my spinach and goat cheese, but we also sample Tiger Mountain Viognier with some Georgia shrimp (perfect with the wine's citrus overtones). Chantelle is "testing" several wines on her weeknight guests, so we get to taste a French Chardonnay as well, a Jadot Pouilly Fuisse. To our delight, Chantelle and some of the guests think our Georgia grown Viognier more perfectly complements the Georgia shrimp.

For the main course, I would love the sea bass but decide I want to have a wonderful red of Chantelle's choice, so I order the quail with bacon bread pudding. John chooses the hangar steak with a Merlot mushroom sauce. We enjoy a Merryvale Cabernet Sauvignon although Chantelle thinks our French style Malbec would also suit quail or duck. John is especially pleased about that because far too many Malbec drinkers are looking for the full-bodied, higher alcohol (and less expensive) Malbecs from Argentina.

Dessert, a crème brulee for me and a lemon pudding cake with strawberries for John, comes with a French Muscat dessert wine. In the end, Chantelle promises to order three of our wines: Viognier, Malbec, and Touriga Nacional.

Before we leave, she asks her maître' d to take a photo of the three of us. I'm certain I look as fat as I feel, but this is a photo that will go on our web site regardless.

We are elated with our success as we walk back to the car in the soft summer evening air. "Only in the South," says our daughter Lisa, who grew up accustomed to the briskness of Colorado summer evenings, "does the soft air caress your whole body."

"The Dining Room lives up to its elegant reputation," I say to John as we climb into the stuffy car. (Thankfully, John is always conscious of the long drive home and never drinks all of any of the wines poured.) "I suppose," he replies, "but you know we spent more on dinner than a case of our wine will cost the Ritz."

"Don't be a spoiler," I say. "The Ritz is about bragging rights. Think of it as the 'ripple effect' when it comes to establishing our image with upscale buyers."

"I'll celebrate when the wines are delivered and paid for," he murmurs skeptically.

"I'll write Chantelle a thank you tomorrow," I say, "on my new chartreuse note cards with the tiny grapes at the top—the stationery you thought was so extravagant."

Sure enough, weeks go by with no order from Chantelle, and I try to think of a graceful reason to call her once more. Finally, I decide I can call and offer some specific times for her to join us for lunch in the vineyards since she mentioned how much she wants to see and feel the vines. I telephone and discover she is in New York, so I leave a message. Almost a month goes by, and I am discouraged. To make matters worse, I sense John's "I told you so" attitude when the subject of the Ritz comes up.

"Well, there are other Ritz Carltons we could try," I say to John defensively.

"Yeah, but the Buckhead Dining Room is the only five-star one," he replies.

Then, one day, out of the blue again, I receive a call from Chantelle on our home phone. I felt lucky to be at home when she called with the order we had been waiting for—three wines, two cases.

"Hey, we're actually up one case, even considering the dinner," John teases, but I am elated that we have swung our first five-star listing.

I try not to sound overanxious and tell Chantelle the wine will be delivered the following week—knowing that I have a longstanding lunch appointment in Buckhead with a lawyer friend. I make sure the duplicate invoice form has our color logo (John and our winery manager are prone to copy it in black and white) with no typos or spots on the form, a recurring problem for some of our hurried staff. I don my favorite (and only) St. John knit dress with jacket for lunch and plan to stop by the Ritz and deliver the wine personally beforehand. While I'd hate for Chantelle to discover that I am also the delivery woman, I know from her instructions where the wine must be delivered and which office in the caverns of the Ritz writes the checks. Fortunately for a small winery, the alcohol laws demand that wine be paid for upon delivery.

When I arrive at the Ritz side entry, with a dolly and two cases of wine, the doorman has mercy on me and loads it on the service elevator headed to the sub-sub basement. I'm accompanied by the laundry detail. Pulling the dolly along the narrow corridor in my high heels, I spot the small window at the cashier's office and the receiving dock without a hitch.

I finally get back upstairs, this time sharing the freight elevator with a janitor and a large recycling bin. When I round the corner of the ground floor into the sunshine and stately décor of the main lobby, I cannot help but dab my eyes. What is this? I am not a weeping woman—really I am not. I sit down momentarily, tissue in hand. I wish John were with me, but I can't reach him on his cell. I gaze at the shiny brass doors and the giant lobby chandelier and think about the first scrawny plants, sticks really, that we groveled around in the dirt to plant at the farm when everyone, even our own children, thought we were nuts. Now, I can close my eyes at any time and envision the lush green vines, the bright tangerine roses, our Tuscan-style home on a vineyard hillside against Tiger Mountain. I can explain to guests the transformation of a little cement block creamery building—where we made our first wine with only a room air conditioner and an old apple press—into a triple-gabled stucco winery with yellow awnings, purple shutters, and glass rain leaders (instead of gutters) that give it a touch of class. The contemporary metal sculpture I covet for the tasting room patio is yet to be, but metal tables we have, complete with chartreuse and purple umbrellas. We're not sedate old world and we're not slick Napa. We're just a farm winery in little ol' Tiger, Georgia. And now we're fit for a five-star.

18

End the Commute, Not the Marriage

As the business grows, so does the workload. John manages the vineyards and his medical practice, but much of the tedious paperwork, the staffing headaches, and certainly the marketing, fall to me. There is the unending challenge of making visits to our winery and vineyards an aesthetic experience—as in abundant flowers and few weeds, even with too little help. We are on overload, and we are cross with each other. There is partnership friction too, an age-old problem for small businesses that involve joint ownership.

I arrive after dark from Atlanta most Friday nights only to face an exhausting schedule of tours, guests in and out—sometimes for dinner—flowers to arrange for the tasting room and cheese to buy although we alternate those responsibilities every other weekend with our partners. Getting John down to events with my Atlanta friends is a lost cause. When they invite us to dinner or a concert on a Saturday night in the city, even I am not ready for an extra trip to the city and back.

Then there is the marketing, most of which I'm pretty good at. At least I know to meet deadlines when publications call and to be ready to e-mail photos or get John to do a winemaker interview spontaneously. At this stage of our winery life, we'd never turn down free publicity, no matter if with an obscure weekly publication or a radio show unknown to most of the world.

We don't exactly have *Wine Spectator* calling, but *Southern Living*, the most popular lifestyle magazine in the South, wants to do a story on our vineyard and home. It will be a great chance to give Shelly the credit she deserves for our unique house-in-the-vineyard design. The magazine's reporter and photographer will interview us and shoot pictures at harvest, a whole year ahead—to be published the following fall. But given the increasing frequency at which John and I are snapping at each other while we are both so stressed, will we still be together?

I get up at 6:00 A.M. no matter what time I go to bed. Most mornings I can see the mist rising from the pond when I step out the front door; I can watch a few deer scampering close to the woods. How in the world can I feel so irritable amidst all of this beauty?

The vineyard and winery have become so much work that it's not fun anymore. Whatever happened to the carefree, on-a-lark spirit that made it all reality?

At midnight on Saturday, following a small dinner party for six wonderful friends—yes, we have made real and lasting friends here—I am sitting at my computer in the study answering e-mails. Worse yet, I'm printing some of them out for John, the most agitating part of my days and nights at the farm.

John does not e-mail. Why? Because he doesn't want to.

But who else has that luxury? He does financial spreadsheets on my computer just fine. But he claims he's always going to choose digging in the dirt over pounding on a keyboard inside or even on some electronic device outside. (He was the last person in our family and in our business to agree to carry a cell phone although he'd used a pager for his medical calls for ages.)

I hear a lizard scampering across the screen on my study window, and I peer out at the full moon with fluffy clouds darting in and out of its shimmering light. The Touriga Nacional vines near our courtyard are glistening with tiny drops from an evening shower, and the curls on the paperbark maple tree just outside my study window are shimmering in a soft breeze.

John has been in bed at least an hour, after washing a few pots and pans for me. I go to the front door, sit down on the outside steps, and stare at the silhouette of the barn. Beams of light dance on the metal roof. Beyond is the familiar dark line of mountain ridges that I could close my eyes and trace with great precision from now to the end of time. The night is calm. In fact, the nighttime view from our library tower is stunning—dappled sky, blue mountains, deep green vines with the barn behind, its white trim outlining its magnificent structure. The old silo, covered in vines, is visible too in the moonlight, making me wish I were viewing the vineyards from its top, impossible to reach.

Why do I so seldom pause to enjoy the extraordinary beauty and calm that envelops our farm? Why aren't John and I walking among the vines at sunset? We found time for those things not so very long ago.

Ironically, before I go to bed, I open one more e-mail. It's from a former high school pal in Atlanta who visited us with some of my other classmates recently. "How is everything up there in your little piece of paradise?" she writes. I close the e-mail. Maybe I'll answer her tomorrow. When I wake up the next morning, our bedroom is washed in orange and pink—another magnificent sunrise. John turns off the alarm and we snuggle quietly, watching the brilliant colors replaced by a sunny blue sky.

"I've got to get this bedroom finished," I murmur, knowing my intention to replace the small walnut double bed we've slept in for three decades is a sore point with John. Of course, it looks ridiculous in the otherwise contemporary setting. "I thought you liked a mix of the old and new, for character," John replies.

"When it works, I do, but this doesn't," I respond, sweeping my arm across the dark wood bed and antique organ a patient insisted John have. It's an instrument he enjoys playing from time to time though he only knows how to play hymns on it.

"Shelly and I have designed a bed with an asymmetrical headboard that Peter Bull has promised to build for me," I say, reaching over to turn off the alarm. Peter, who built our kitchen, seldom agrees to build any piece that is to be painted. He's a wood craftsman extraordinaire, and he's in love with the feel and texture and natural grain of all kinds of wood. But for me, he says he'll build this wood bed that will be painted a washed white.

John looks crushed after I finish babbling about the bed as well as the bedside tables I'm making—with help—from glass blocks. He looks almost as sad as he did a few days ago when one of his longtime fishing buddies died. I know how attached he is to the old bed. We bought it at an auction when he was in his urology residency in Missouri. We paid less than twenty dollars for it, only to spend a couple of hundred to get it lengthened so we could actually get a double bed mattress in it.

I understand his sentimentality and promise to save the bed for one of the children. I decide back pain is the best way to approach a new bed. "Well, we both have suffered sore backs lately," I add. "We really need a new mattress, and queen size will definitely be more comfortable."

Silence.

I feel guilty, but not for long. The phone rings and Judy says one of us is going to be needed in the tasting room in the afternoon. I volunteer to cover, since I know John wants to work in the vineyard. I sigh, but he doesn't notice. Getting out in the vineyards again on weekends is more and more my impossible dream.

John's still in a sour mood over my bedroom re-do plans. "Yes, one wall will be apple green," I add excitedly as I hang up the phone.

"Puke," he replies.

After the tasting room closes, I scurry back to the house to pack up for the drive to the city. It's dark by the time we grab a quick bite to eat and I am already dreading the long drive.

When I get to the car, John hollers, "Wait." He comes out and gives me a kiss. "You know, we haven't lived together for ten years," he says.

Some five hours later, after I've unpacked and gone through my mail that evening, those words won't go away. I keep hearing them as I crawl into bed in my apartment with my *New York Times*, the city skyline glistening out my twelfth-floor window. The phone rings and it's our California daughter, Lisa.

"Sorry to be calling so late," she says, "I'm always forgetting our three-hour difference."

"It's not so late," I reply laughing. "I'm not anywhere close to going to sleep." Indeed, I am usually asleep over the book review section by now, but I'm still thinking about John's parting words at the farm.

"I just talked to Dad," she says, "What's the matter with him? He sounds—well, he just sounds *down*."

"We're both spread way too thin," I respond. "I guess he's just super tired."

"I wish there were some way for you to be at the farm more to help him," she says. This makes me feel bad, since Lisa is the daughter who urged me to follow my heart and my writing when I moved to Atlanta and started our cross-country commute that went on for three years.

"I know you love your writing," she says, "and we all love your column, Mom. But isn't there a way to telecommute?"

"Are you kidding?" I respond. "Not if I want to keep my column and not if I want to be on the editorial board," I reply. "The *Journal-Constitution* has precious few part-timers and none who are allowed their own column. In the news business, things happen without warning—and you've got to be on the scene to respond if you want to be a significant player."

"Maybe it's just a matter then of hiring more help at the farm," Lisa says, and we wander off to other conversation.

But when I hang up, I'm even more distressed at the state of John's and my situation—and, well, our deteriorating relationship. We've both worked hard and are afraid to leave our day jobs, of course. Much of the vineyard and winery really is fun when we're not constantly overwhelmed, but we've been staying overwhelmed. We both love the land itself, what we produce from it, and sharing a taste of our special piece of earth with others. The marketing and selling and tending and pouring and wining and dining have gotten in the way of that simple joy we started with.

It is almost midnight when I put down the *New York Times* I've tried to read as I always do in bed on Sunday night. I pick up the phone and call John. I wake him, of course.

I tell him I've made a great decision: I'm coming to the farm full time, maybe by the end of the year.

"Wait," he says, "we need to talk about that. I don't know if you'll be happy in Tiger full time. And what about your column? Let's take some time to talk this over next weekend. I've got to be in surgery at 7 A.M." His voice trails off. "Why did you decide to break that news in the middle of the night?" Now there's that edge in his voice that I hate. I am silent.

"I thought you'd be happy to know. But, okay, we'll talk about it. Love you."

I turn out the light and turn on public radio too for the sake of some soothing classical music. Normally I know on Sunday night what the subject of my Tuesday column will be, but this night I am blank. The column is not what's on my mind. John is.

John and I discuss my moving to the farm several times over the next few weeks, but he still worries I will regret giving up my position at the paper. Meanwhile, another harvest comes and goes. I barely squeeze in two long weekends to help. The editor, Ron Martin, who was responsible for opening the door for me to a whole new career in my early fifties, retires, and there are many changes in the newsroom and on the editorial board. Martin was one of those rare editors who cared about good writing above all. My column, which was running in the Sunday section, was moved to Tuesdays even before his departure. I submit my letter of resignation from the board in November and plan to depart December 15. John continues to have his doubts about my adjustment to living full-time in Tiger and makes it clear he'll spend no more than the sporadic time of the past few years in Atlanta with me. My last column at the paper is one of gratitude to my readers mixed with what I'll miss on a daily basis about Atlanta, my intriguing hometown:

Country Life Won't Erase Love for City

Three blanketed figures lay in the doorway between Michael's Café and the Downtown Dental Clinic on a soft November night as I left my Marietta Street office. I walked toward the sparkling towers of Centennial Olympic Park—a few blocks and worlds away from the homeless men.

Across the street, CNN beamed stories from Iraq, while down at city hall, the mayor dreamed of a piece of the Bagdad reconstruction pie to fund Atlanta's corroded sewers. Yes, indeed, I'm going to miss the daily throb of life in my hometown, a city that is still becoming. Though I'm not moving very far away, returning now and then isn't the same as being part of a city's soul....

I'll miss the marquee of the historic Rialto Theater where I've thrilled to Wynton Marsalis and some of the world's best jazz. Oh-so-many-moons ago, in the balcony of the Rialto, I giggled with a first date as we watched "House of Wax" while balancing 3-D cardboard glasses on our noses.

I'll miss the reliable magic of the Atlanta skyline when I drive back from our mountain home on Sunday nights. From the Spring Street viaduct, which blocks the ugly parking decks below, it is a panorama of contemporary castle tops, pyramids and turrets of light....

You see, I know what has changed about Atlanta and what never will.... Atlanta is a weaving of textures and patterns that will take you in any direction you want to go. Like an adolescent trying to become an adult, it's a city still acting out in a state where flag fights are a little like school cafeteria food fights. It's a city where leaders fuss about renaming the airport, then act like grown ups to build a symphony hall.

I'm moving away from my intriguing hometown—to Tiger, population 316. I'll hike mountain trails instead of jogging in Piedmont Park. And I'll still write for the *Atlanta Journal-Constitution* once in a while from our North Georgia home.

My column will not appear again on these pages, but the lively opinions of the most creative bunch of professionals I've ever encountered will continue to prod and provoke. Over the past decade, I have been blessed to hear from readers—angry, thoughtful, caring and a little crazy. They have all enriched my life. But now, two roads diverge in a yellow wood, and I'm taking the country one, back to a mountain boy I've only hooked up with on weekends for the past ten years.

I'm on the road to Tiger.[13]

[13] *Atlanta Journal-Constitution*, 25 November 2003, A-19.

19

Mornings with the Streetwalkers

The pastoral views from every room of our home are a soothing way to start the day. But soothing doesn't last long in our Tiger home. My office opens onto the kitchen and family room, wonderful angled spaces filled with light, but there are no doors; anyone who comes into the house can wander into my office as well. We are seldom without unannounced visitors—relatives, farm and vineyard workers, or neighbors. John's relatives, colorful and interesting, are usually bearing garden produce or some yummy homemade cake to share with us. Our two regular vineyard workers come in, as we have encouraged them to do, to get ice or a cold drink and to ask John questions about the work schedule for the particular day or week. If John is seeing patients or doing surgery, as he is two or three days a week, I try to answer the worker questions and greet the unannounced visitors. I resent the unscheduled interruptions, but this is life in the unhurried small town of Tiger, after all, and I need to get used to it.

Before leaving my post at the paper, I contracted to write a series I'd suggested about the mistaken policy at the North Georgia maximum security prison that mandates that juvenile offenders "walk across the yard' to be housed with adult prisoners once they turn sixteen. Rape, abuse, and racial gang fights become a way of life for the youth inside the walls. The

North Georgia prison is not far away, but the series demands hours of research, dozens of phone calls each day, and weeks of concentrated writing. I soon find my home office environment is not conducive to any of that. I conduct heartbreaking interviews one by one in a windowless room at the prison with ten carefully selected juvenile inmates. When I return home to glorious vistas and wildlife at the farm, I can't help but wonder what it does to the soul of youth never to be outdoors except in a barbed wire and cement lot for all of the teenage years with no hope of parole—the requirements of Georgia's mandatory sentencing for commission of violent offenses. One twenty-four-year-old offender, imprisoned at age fifteen for ten years, tells me all he wants to do when he gets out is to lie down on the ground and look at the stars, which he hasn't seen in nine years.[14] I am grateful for the magical night sky that is mine to savor every night—minus city light "pollution."

What gives me chills every time I drive through the gates of the ominous prison is that it is named for one of John's relatives—a man who served on several state commissions. It's the Arrendale State Prison. Arrendale, John's mom's maiden name, is John's middle name. We once considered naming the vineyards the old English original surname, *Arundel Vineyards*. I'm glad we didn't. The Arrendale relatives also own a huge poultry operation in the area. While all of the various ventures the large family undertook are worthy, neither a prison nor a chicken business lends itself to a fine wine image.

---

[14] "Throwing Away the Key," *Atlanta Journal-Constitution*, 28 March 2004, F 1-5.

During the time I am writing the articles on the horrors of housing youthful offenders in a maximum security prison with hardened adult criminals, one teenager is raped and murdered. I finish the series, and later on, state officials enact a new policy, which sends young adult inmates to a separate facility. I win a couple of awards for investigative journalism, but writing from home is an ever-interrupted struggle that I am certain I don't want to undertake again. The biggest surprise is that my husband is testy about the long hours of research and reporting that take me away from the daily marketing demands of the winery even though I explain that this is a one-time assignment and that future writing projects won't be as time-consuming.

"Why are you so upset about the time this writing assignment is taking?" I fume to him over a cheeseburger at the Tiger Food Mart. "After all, I wasn't even here to carry out these duties for years."

"Because now you *are* here," he says, "and we're on the cusp of making this vineyard and winery a going operation, even a profitable one."

"Aren't we supposed to enjoy the daily doing of it?" I reply. "You know I can't love life in Tiger if I have to give up my writing totally."

It is a fruitless conversation, and we both know it.

Nevertheless, John and I are enjoying our renewed relationship, including the recovery of our dinnertime conversations each evening. The downside is that we are also stumbling all over each other. While he's settled rather well into his part-time country medical practice, John seems to expect me to make up those hours he's losing in the vineyards and winery while he's practicing medicine—a couple of days' worth each week.

"Can you make these shipping labels online and get three marketing packets put together by noon—and do you mind calling that wine shop in Gainesville to see if we can get a re-order?"

I am still writing a few short pieces for the paper and for a magazine, but the interruptions never end. "Where did I put the keys to the bottling room—tell the label people when they call that we need 28,000 back labels by Friday week...." Tell me to prune twenty-five vines by sundown and I would happily do it, but this daily minutia is smothering me.

"I told you the electrician said he'd stop by sometime this week to look at the motion lights at the winery—no I don't know when, just one day this week," he adds as he revs up the gator in the garage so he couldn't possibly hear me reply that I may not be just hanging around the house every single minute of every day.

It occurs to me belatedly that the last thing I ever wanted to do is to be in business with my husband.

We have always pursued separate professional paths. John still operates with that small town handshake and laid back notion of scheduling. I'm trained as a lawyer, and I want appointments certain, a deadline and a written contract.

Despite my frustrations with running a small business from home, I relish the wonders of the farm and its seasons in a way I never had time for when I was racing to and from Atlanta. I rise early and so does the mist at the pond. I take walks to admire the wildlife, the cattails, the surprise patches of colorful wild flowers on the banks. I delight in seeing a graceful white egret or hearing the flapping wings of a low-flying blue heron splashing down to scoop up a fish for breakfast. But my walks get shorter and shorter as winery duties left undone from the day before beckon. I have a hard time putting them aside for my cherished farm walks when I know I can be productive and uninterrupted at the computer in those early hours. I fret after clipping purple asters at the pond as I take a shortcut through the hayfields back to the house. Glorious though the flowers and wildlife are, I should be home answering those twenty-two e-mails left from yesterday.

After a couple of hours at the computer, I take a mid-morning break and head to Fromage in Clayton, a delightful café that also carries aged cheeses that are perfect for our tasting room: Spanish Manchego, French Morbier, and double crème brie. When I run errands in Clayton or stop at the grocery, I'm always aware, and gratefully so, that everything I need for everyday life is within a five-block radius of Clayton's one traffic light. It's not like I had to drive through stop-and-go city traffic to more than one shopping area.

I'm still attached to the tiny Andy's Market even though I can't always find a ripe avocado or prewashed greens there. Only at Andy's, though, can I buy local water-ground corn meal in brown paper sacks tied with string, old fashioned hominy grits, and jars of beautiful sourwood honey with the honeycomb in them—items that more than make up for the supermarket offerings. Andy's must be one of the few markets left on earth where my groceries are taken to my car while I'm still writing a check. Andy and his employees know their customers' vehicles, including our farm truck.

This morning, I run into my friend Betsy Fowler in Andy's parking lot. She's wearing exercise clothes, and I ask if she's been to the gym. "No," Betsy says with a laugh, "I'm always out early, even before light, with the Streetwalkers. You ought to join us sometime."

Now I know Betsy is the very proper wife of a physician who was in medical school with my husband long ago—so I know there's more to this story.

"So who are the other Streetwalkers, and what time are you out?" I ask.

"Oh, three of us meet at 7:00 every weekday morning and walk three miles. We meet in the Baptist church parking lot downtown; it's a good place for 'Streetwalkers' to gather," she adds in a teasing tone. She mentions Rebekah Krivsky and Sylvia Turner, both of whom have been to our winery numerous times.

Feeling guilty about my erratic exercise schedule, I tell Betsy I may just show up for some morning jaunts. My farm walks are getting shorter and shorter, and I only go sporadically to a 6 P.M. aerobics class that often interferes with evening wine events—though Dolly Ramey, the instructor, who holds the class at the middle school gym, is tougher than any LA Fitness teacher I had in the city.

The next morning, I am greeted with a warm welcome when I arrive in the Clayton Baptist Church parking lot to join the Streetwalkers' lively jaunt through downtown Clayton. We walk to the police station and back and on to Stekoa Creek, past the huge, ugly car lots on the new highway and back up the hill by Regions Bank. Part of the route takes us past the Civic Center where we can check the time and temperature screen on our way back to the church lot. It's an invigorating time; much of the conversation is centered on local people and events, a close-up of the Rabun County world I've only begun to know. All three of my walking friends, well-educated and well-traveled women, have lived in Clayton all of their adult lives and raised their families in Rabun County.

John and I are planning a trip to Italy in late fall, and I soon discover I can learn more about Tuscany from Rebekah and Betsy than I can find in a travel book. And Sylvia, a nurse who also likes to garden, invariably comes up with the names of plants and shrubs I'm trying to find and cultivate. When Rebekah returns from a trip to Switzerland and other spots in Europe, she brings all of us small gifts. I learn that this is Streetwalker tradition: every time any one of the group goes on a significant trip, presents from the visit are in order for the rest. Betsy tells the story of when the three of them traveled to New York and donned their SWOW (Streetwalkers of the World) T-shirts when they visited the *Today* show window at NBC. It all seems a far cry from discussions of legal matters with women lawyer friends over box lunches in a high rise office building or endless editorial board "endorsement" interviews with political candidates, not that those weren't interesting and challenging. But I am slowly discovering the joys of small-town life and the fascinating people who live around me. Living in the country is a do-it-yourself deal, with nature's delights the reward.

"Ahhh, life in Tiger," I say to my daughter Shelly, who calls after I've just discovered our well has a broken pump when I return from hauling the trash, bottles and cans in the back of the pick up to the dump and recycling center. (In addition to no Starbucks in Tiger, there's no garbage pick up.) Just when I start to complain though, two tiny goldfinches show up to play tag in the perennial sunflowers outside my kitchen window, flitting in and out of large yellow petals that are their perfect match. Even days that aren't sunny in Tiger *are*.

I have always favored yellows, reds, and oranges, the so-called warm colors, so it's no surprise to John that I discover a used pick-up truck, a yellow Ford Ranger, that I covet for driving around town. "It matches the winery awning," I tell him as he rolls his eyes.

"Why not go for a taxi or a school bus?" he replies, but I know he's vulnerable because he's noticed my down mood lately, attributable to so little time for writing or city visits.

"Well, the Streetwalkers voted unanimously that I should have the yellow truck from the moment I spotted it," I plead. "Just think how cool it will look with a Tiger Mountain Vineyards logo tag on the front."

Actually, the Streetwalkers helped me spot the truck when we walked by the car lot one morning. It seemed to jump out at all of us as perfect for a farm winery owner. A few weeks before, I had accordion-pleated the front of my old

Mercedes when I rear-ended the car in front of me at a red turn signal I failed to see at a stoplight that was green for through traffic. The used but spotless yellow Ford Ranger must surely be a middle ground between his ugly farm truck and the cool Toyota Tundra—the scoffed-at "latte crowd" truck he wouldn't consider because the truck bed was too small for hauling farm equipment.

"I'm sure someone is going to grab it," I warn John later in the week when the Streetwalkers suggest that I should at least go drive it.

"Didn't you say it's a stick shift with manual windows and doors?" he asks. "Be patient, the price will come down." He finally suggests I go drive it anyhow, and I can hardly wait to do so. When the salesman gives me the keys, he tells me he must copy my driver's license before I can drive off the lot. While he's gone, I hear his name as he's being paged. He returns to tell me sheepishly that someone has just put a down payment on the truck. It's sold after all.

I am not just disappointed but downright mad with my husband for causing me to dally around about snatching up the perfect farm winery truck.

"I'm going to look for a yellow Jeep instead," I tell John that evening as I huff and puff around the house. "You can't buy a Jeep," he says. "We can't write a Jeep off as farm equipment."

A few days later, I return late one evening from some appointments in Atlanta. John greets me in a dour mood. "Sit down," he says. "I have some terrible news."

I am certain something bad has happened to one of the children.

"What is it?" I say anxiously.

"The yellow truck is back," he declares with a sigh.

"What do you mean, it's 'back'?"

"The salesman called today to say the young couple who bought it returned to trade it in because they couldn't get a baby seat to fit in it."

The next morning, there it is, clean and shiny and parked at the winery. There's a key in it and a note from the salesman saying I should drive it for the day. My first stop is Andy's Market—and while I am browsing the soup aisle, I hear a familiar voice. It's Rebekah, laughing as she walks towards me.

"I don't really need to shop," she says, "but when I drove by and saw the yellow truck in the parking lot, I decided I'd better go in and see who bought Martha's truck."

By the time I recount the story to her, including John's dismay over the truck's return, I have several nearby shoppers laughing too.

That evening John follows me when I drive the truck back to the Ford dealer and offers before we leave to buy it for me himself. While he's groused around about it, I can tell he really wants me to have it. He knows I've been in a funk lately over our ever-consuming business-out-of-home, and he's sure the truck is going to change my mood.

He's right. I put a couple of Eliza Gilkyson folk music CDs in it, roll down the windows and feel free as a farm girl should, driving it over the hills and through the vineyards at sunset.

"My yellow truck has made me feel ten years younger," I tell him giddily. "Come for a ride."

"No thanks—I'm not riding in that shoebox," he replies with a grin. "I'm surprised you like the stick shift. I mean, except for the garish color, it's a no-frills truck, and frills usually appeal to you."

"Well, isn't farming all about getting back to the basics?" I reply, and he gives me one of his big bear hugs.

20

The Frost Dragon and a Record Freeze

It's an unusually gray winter, and I long for the drama of a Colorado-style snowstorm. Instead, low gray clouds hang in hooded shapes, roiling around high enough at midday to allow a peek at the tip of Tiger Mountain. They descend on the farm again at dusk. My trips to the city become less frequent. I am committed to honing my pruning skills this winter, so out I go with John and a worker almost every day to prune vines. I've been pruning on and off for years now, but it's an art—and I haven't mastered it to the extent John has. I probably never will.

For your father, it's innate, I tell the children, but for me, it's a steep learning curve. Though the temperatures aren't even below freezing, there is a constant dampness that chills to the bone. We tackle the Viognier first because John feels it is the greatest challenge; many of the vines have weak canes and need restructuring.

"Remember not to leave more than seven or eight shoots per cordon," John says again, as I tackle a snarly vine with canes going in all directions. Unlike my delinquent subject of the moment, though, most of the canes reach upward in graceful swirls. I reluctantly cut them to short stubby shoots jutting out from horizontal cordons along the wire. I already know to cut each of the young canes to only two buds. When

I end up with ten two-bud shoots on a single cordon, I inevitably holler to John for advice on which of the extras to lop off entirely. And I am usually wrong in my proposed choices. I have chosen a shoot that is coming out underneath the wire instead of on top, or I have selected to save shoots that are too close to each other. John wants them spaced out. Then, there is the scary decision to cut off an entire thick cordon or arm that is too weak to sustain new growth and bring a cane over from the opposite side to the weak side in order to structure a new arm. (But what if there is no cane long or strong enough to do that?) Sometimes John will leave both the old and new tied to the horizontal wire to see which turns out to be healthiest come spring bud break. He'll cut one off then.

"Didn't our Italian winegrower friend tell us we should think of one vine, one bottle?" I ask John. "I mean, given that one vine in our divided trellis system produces four cordons, we're talking about twenty-one or more bunches of grapes—that's way more than one bottle, isn't it?"

"Seldom is," John replies. "You'd have to get perfect berry set and beautiful clusters from every single bud for that to be true. That's not going to happen."

I feel smug that I finally understand about berry set, which occurs after the grapes bloom in spring. Their non-showy "bloom" resembles the wispy white seed head of a dandelion, and only after the bloom do berries form that will grow to maturity. If the weather is too wacky and there's no bloom, there may be some tiny hard berries, but they won't mature. One spring we had a hailstorm that damaged some blooms and cut into our usual production.

"The one vine-one bottle notion also depends on the grape variety," John continues. "Viognier has small berries and doesn't produce many excessive clusters. The opposite is true of Tannat, of course, which is so prolific, with huge berries and tight, gigantic clusters. You know that—it's why we go back though those Tannat vines several times and drop so many clusters in summer."

We continue pruning in silence. The unpruned vines, with their long, willowy canes still intact, project intricate patterns across the vineyards in the late afternoon sun. I think of them as my winter cathedral, arched arms lifted to the heavens as if in prayer.

Pruning is great therapy—getting rid of the superfluous, eliminating all but what is essential to sustain life. But after two and a half hours, my fingers are tingling and the wind comes up. I take a break for hot tea, but not John. He will prune until sunset. Pruning is his favorite aspect of grape growing. "It's where great wines begin," he tells every new vineyard worker.

After a week of gray drizzle, I am looking forward to our dinner tomorrow evening with "The Rabun L's"—two couples, Bob and Margaret Hatcher, Jeff and Jeanne Kronsnoble, along with John and me—who share similar liberal political views in our otherwise super-conservative county. We also share books we've read.

Tomorrow night we are going to the Kronsnobles' home on Tiger Creek, an earthy, elegant stone and wood structure with a balcony on the tumbling creek waters. On one side of the house, a stone fireplace on the deck lures us even in winter. Jeff, who likes to cook, is an artist who taught art at the University of South Florida for many years and before that, trained to become a Catholic priest. He has also been known to burst forth with a liturgical chant before dinner, to our delight.

We and the Hatchers look forward to our regular visits upstairs to Jeff's studio to view his latest works. Jeanne owns Main Street Gallery in Clayton, which features unusual pottery, jewelry, and folk art. A few years ago, Jeanne's gallery was written up in the *New York Times* arts section. When our daughters come to the farm, they can hardly wait to visit the gallery. There's nothing like it in the city, they say.

"It's been a wonderfully mild winter," Margaret comments over Jeff's slow cooked pork and Jeanne's perfect risotto.

John pours some of our rich, dark Tannat, and adds, "Unfortunately." We grape growers need cold temperatures to kill off all of the varmints that attack our grapes, the fly that carries the dreaded Pierce's disease, and the Japanese beetles that cold never kills but bitter cold may deter a bit.

"Wait now, John, you'll admit it's been great for golf," says Bob. He and Margaret are both avid golfers, but in Rabun County golfing is usually limited to April though November.

"How would we know?" I chime in. "Golf is a long-ago luxury of our pre-vineyard life." It's true we played golf in Colorado but not much in recent years.

John pledges to go golfing the very next week with Jeff and Bob, and the weather continues to be unseasonably warm. The temperatures, in fact, are record highs for a Rabun County March, and our buds begin to pop out two weeks ahead of their normal bud break. We are always nervous about early bud break because of the threat of late frost in April. Sure enough, freezing temperatures are forecast for our North Georgia mountains come the second week of April.

"This is serious," John says, looking over my shoulder at the ten-day forecast on the computer screen. "Looks like we're in for a hard freeze day after tomorrow. We'd better get ready."

Some of our fellow Georgia wine growers have purchased motorized windmills they can roll around to different spots in their vineyards. One even hired a helicopter or two the last time we suffered a late frost, something *so* California that we snickered about it until we learned that his grapes had remained frost-free. John has never been convinced that the rolling hills of our vineyards are configured quite right for windmills to be effective, and we certainly don't feel we can afford helicopters, which cost thousands per hour. Our options are limited to a Frost Dragon and smudge pots. The Frost Dragon is a propane-propelled gismo that attaches to the tractor. The only time we've really used it was two years ago in April when temperatures dipped to 28 degrees. It was pretty effective, but that was a frost, not a freeze, John reminds me.

In the dark of night, the Frost Dragon looks like a ball of fire rolling through the vineyards, the wide ring in back exhibiting bright flames. It actually blows hot air out both sides as it travels between the rows of vines. John and one farm worker are the only ones trained to run it. If you drive it too fast, it's not effective, and if you drive it too slowly, it could scorch the leaves.

We ordered the second-hand smudge pots online and have never used them. A few of them are worn and unsteady. But the day before this awful cold blast is to come down upon us, John, Coach, another worker, and I run around placing the smudge pots at strategic spots at the ends of sloping rows of grapes. It's almost dusk before we decide to put the diesel fuel in.

"Isn't that diesel smoke going to pollute the whole valley?" I ask Coach.

"You bet," he chuckles, "but this is an agricultural emergency to my way of thinking."

John shakes his head reticently. "If we put the diesel in the pots, we're going to have to burn them no matter what," he says, "even if it turns out by some miracle that we don't need them. We can't move them full of fuel."

As the sun begins to sink, our neighbor Bob Massee from Tiger Mountain Orchards pulls up in his truck just as John is getting the Frost Dragon ready. Massee, we always say, knows more about farming and weather than all of us put together.

"Wish we could at least get a little puff of wind, John, to stir this cold air around some. This still air's no good."

"What's your best advice, Bob?" John asks, knowing Massee has weathered many spring frosts and freezes at his Tiger apple orchards.

"I'll tell you, John. You just need to get yourself some jelly jar caps, pour water in 'em, and put them on top of a few of these trellis posts. I'd check 'em about midnight and every hour after," he says. "If they start getting slushy and icy, you'd better get on out and rev up your Dragon."

"We've had a lot of high tech advice, but that may be the best," I say to John, laughing, as we walk back up the hill when Massee drives away. I run in the house and find some jelly jar lids and take them to John. "You're going to follow Bob's advice, aren't you?" John nods and heads back towards the vineyards with the jar lids and a can of water.

We eat a bowl of chili I've made with some of our Norton wine and some wheat bread for an early supper. (I add Norton, which has a strong acid structure, to almost every meat sauce I make these days, fancy or casual.) John talks with our friend Evan Heckel on the phone, promising to telephone him when we head out tonight. I get the flashlights ready on the kitchen table, and we both slip into our long underwear, leaving our warm pants, jackets, gloves, and hats ready to put on later in the night.

We go to bed about 9:30, but it's impossible for me to sleep that early. My eyes are wide open as I ponder the Big Dipper in the inky, cloudless sky from our bedroom windows. Just as Massee warned, it's still as can be. If we weren't dreading the temperature drop and the fate of our delicate spring buds, it would be a romantic winter night—crystal clear with the new moon a perfect cradle above.

I toss and turn.

"Oh, we'll get through it," John says, putting his arm around me. "Don't be so stressed."

"I hope you told Coach not to come over," I say.

"Yep—I insisted that he wait until morning to help. He's getting too old for night duty, for sure."

Before I know it, John has dozed off while I'm still staring at the stars dancing above the graceful profile of Raven's Wing Mountain in the distance. Magnificent as the beauty of it all is just now, I know that a few clouds and a little wind would be our better angels against a hard freeze. I finally doze a little, but at midnight, the alarm goes off, and we both jump up. I race to the computer to get the local temperature and John turns on the weather channel. "Damn, damn," I hear him mutter, his clothes already on, as he heads out to start the gator and drive toward the barn to ready the Frost Dragon.

"Call Beto," he hollers, "and Evan, too." Beto is our farm worker who knows how to drive the Dragon and Evan, our engineer friend—calm and upbeat even in the direst circumstances—is committed to helping us light the smudge pots and track the temperatures in the different vineyards. He has helped us fix everything on the farm, from the tractor to my computer hard drive that I once thought I'd lost. Evan and his wife, Ginny, are an essential part of our winery family. Ginny organizes pourers for many of our events, takes great photos, and spends her time on carefully selected community and church projects, heading the Episcopal Outreach program for the Atlanta Diocese. Ginny has also introduced me to talented local potters and to her favorite folk music. It's because of Ginny that I started collecting folk music for my yellow truck—an ideal fit for my Ford Ranger pick-up's young spirit. I leave all of our classical music for our family car.

When Evan arrives, he and I divide our smudge pot lighting while John and Beto take turns on the Frost Dragon. It's 2:00 A.M., and I shine my flashlight on one of the jar lids on the trellis post. It's frozen solid.

The vineyard thermometer on another nearby post says 24 degrees—and the coldest part of the night is yet to come. The temperature always dips at early dawn. Thirty minutes later, Evan reads 21 degrees on his thermometer, which is more accurate than the ones attached to the trellis posts. I wave to John as the Frost Dragon rolls past me—I can feel its pulsating hot air and hope it's helping warm the vines a bit. John has on his ski mask hat and his red and blue windbreaker, so he looks like a character out of the *Superman II* movie as he hunches over the wheel of the fiery dragon.

I look up at the dark night sky ablaze with stars and wish for a choir of angels, settling for a humble prayer of my own. We have worked so hard on our vines this year. Their canopies are near perfect—their tiny chartreuse leaves the symbol of new life at its most vibrant. Will all of that turn brown? Will our entire season be lost?

It feels lonely in the dark, cold vineyard. As the first dim lights of dawn tiptoe over the mountains in the distance, I see Judy's blue Jeep coming up the road. I run to the house to meet her and turn on the coffee pot. She has brought a beautiful breakfast casserole and is her usual laughing self.

"A hot breakfast will revive you and the vineyards," she declares. Soon John's sister arrives with hot cinnamon rolls. I go outside and flag down John and Beto, telling them to come in for a bite to eat and some hot coffee or tea. John comes first, smut on his face and hands red as can be. He says he doesn't feel safe driving the Dragon with his fuzzy gloves on—shakes his head as he removes his wool ski hat to reveal tussled salt and pepper hair going all directions. I love it that way.

"Go see if you can fetch Evan," John says. I head towards the barn and meet him coming up the hill towards the house.

"You know, Martha," Evan says in a matter-of-fact tone of voice, "I don't really think any of this is doing any good." While Evan shows no emotion in making his depressing declaration, I want to sit down and cry—because I have a sinking feeling with every new streak of light on the vines, that he is right. I nod silently, wishing I could dig a hole in the Tannat vines and curl up in their roots with my lost diamond.

Swirling up from the smudge pots, the gray smoke creates a thin curtain over the vineyards. The phone rings when I get back to the house. It's Janie P. "Hon, have you ever seen such fog?" she asks.

"Janie, I hate to tell you, but it's not foggy at all. The sun is shining above the awful smoke we've created burning smudge pots all night."

"All night!" she exclaims. "Well, bless your heart—now you just go take a nap and it will be all right."

Calls come from the children too. Everyone tries to console, but it's no use. John and I stand at our floor-to-ceiling living room windows and look out on a sunrise that would normally send me running for my camera. This sunrise seems more like the beginning of the end than the beginning of a new day. Our once-pink and fragile buds are brown and drooping. We are totally exhausted. I offer John a cup of hot tea. Ignoring the tea, he just stands at the window. “Maybe you really can’t grow fine wine grapes in North Georgia,” he says.

21

No Starbucks in Tiger

Our gloom over the spring freeze turns to sour moods and cross words in the weeks that follow.

"Look what we've invested in this operation and look at the bottom line," I say harshly to John, having just committed us to two wine dinners in Atlanta. The winery cannot yet afford staff for wine dinners in the city, and our Tiger partners rarely participate in them. It's a hassle to pack the wines, keep them at the proper temperature for the two-hour drive to Atlanta, and to haul back what we don't pour or sell. We talk about retaining a state-wide distributor so all we'd have to do is show up and talk about our wines, but it will take some research to find the right one for a small winery.

"Oh, I know we are supposed to be glad this winery pays its way whether we ever make a dime or not, but we do all of the marketing around the state; you are pounding away in the winery and in the vineyards every day and we still can't afford to hire any staff for marketing or special events. I've had it."

John heads to the back door, loppers in hand—those funny looking long handled clippers he loves. He retorts, "And I beat my brains out at a half-pay rural medical practice so you can live in this house I thought you loved. Not long ago, you actually enjoyed marketing and wine tasting and showing off our wines at nice dinners—but you've lived in a pretend world all of our lives and you still do." His face is red and his thick hair hasn't seen a comb since yesterday, maybe the day before. He looks as discombobulated as he sounds.

I grab a jacket and head out the front door, slamming it behind me. I jog, then walk as fast as I can, to the pond. I want to close my eyes as I pass the Viognier vines with their freeze-burned leaves. I hurry across the hayfield past the awful kudzu hanging on the big oak trees—vines that block the view of the creek that trickles down to the pond. I hate this stretch of the path because I always think about how charming the creek banks could be with wild daisies and asters and a couple of benches under the trees, instead of kudzu, kudzu, kudzu. It winds up the tree limbs and spreads even into the grass. I'm told the Japanese make baskets and weavings of it. I've meant to go to one of the weaving classes staged in a local art gallery to learn something good and artistic about kudzu, but *I hate it.* I often envision what an absolutely gorgeous place the many coves and woods and creek banks on the farm could become—but there is no one on the horizon with the desire or resources to make that happen. I know we should just enjoy the natural beauty of what is and what we have done so far. From the hayfields to the changing seasons on Tiger Mountain to the creek and pond, the farm itself is part of what draws people to our winery, and I can never stop dreaming, it seems, of more ways to enhance its charm.

"Mom, why can't you enjoy what you've already created?" our daughter Lisa asks when I moan about the weed-covered creek banks and the cluttered inside of the barn. "*Country* isn't supposed to be landscaped perfection—who wants to be reminded of the 'burbs, even the upscale 'burbs, when they come to Tiger?" (Always the poet, Lisa recently sent me a card with a bluebird on the front and a Chinese proverb inside that says, "The bird sings not to give a message, but to give a song.")

One of the pressing issues that has made John and me so testy recently is the souring of our winery partnership and the challenge of dissolving it, probably by buying out our current partners—though that will take some outside investors in addition to more of our own resources.

As these things race through my mind, I spot a blue heron rising from the pond, having found his breakfast in the shallow water. There's been no rain since the freeze—breakfast is an easy take for him. The slow, rhythmic flapping of his large wings is sharp contrast to the frantic pace John and I keep. *Slow down, slow down*, they seem to say. It's been so dry since the spring freeze that egret and heron have flocked to the pond to feast on the fish, and there are plenty of fish to feast on. John and I haven't picked up the oars in our little flat bottom boat to fish for bass and blue gill since the children visited last summer. I clip a dozen daffodils springing up near the pond and examine the blueberry bushes. They were badly damaged by the late freeze. I can't remember a summer without blueberries, but we may be coming up on one. I walk back along the gravel road by the barn to avoid running into John, who is performing major surgery on the poor, damaged Viognier. When I arrive at the front door of our house, the phone is ringing. It's one of my favorite wine buyers, Jerry Sinatra, the manager of Fleming's Prime Steakhouse and

Wine Bar in Atlanta where we've agreed to host a wine dinner soon.

"Here's what I'm thinking for some of the pairings—by the way, you don't have a dessert wine do you?"

I want to say, "We may not have any wines at the rate we're going." But I know it will be two years—if we last that long—before we will feel the effects of this year's disaster, at least on our red wine supply.

"No, but we could serve the Cabernet Franc with a berry cobbler if the cobbler's not too sweet," I reply. "But wait—I've got a great idea. What if we offered a barrel taste at the end and had the Cab in a barrel?"

"Fantastic idea," Jerry says. "I'm not sure how we can make that work, but I love it."

"Let me talk to John and get back to you," I add, knowing John will be furious with me for creating such a difficult task as hauling a barrel down to Atlanta and knowing we can't take one that really has wine in it. My idea, though, is to take an empty barrel and put a jug in it near the bung hole. Then we can use the wine thief (the long glass tube) to dip into the carefully placed jug and fill glasses of the guests as a climax to the dinner. They will think the whole barrel is full. And how cool will barrel tasting be in a candlelit room?

The dinner is still a couple of months away. Right now, Fleming's carries only our Malbec but serves it by the glass. Jerry brought his staff up to the vineyards last summer, and they have been excited about our wines ever since. Some of the servers had never seen a wine grape vineyard, and we had a great time. Jerry's wife is the elegant hostess in the five-star

Ritz-Carlton Dining Room in Atlanta. I suspect she had a hand, as did Jerry, in mentioning our local wines favorably to the Ritz sommelier in Buckhead, who chose them.

"How's the reaction to our Malbec, Jerry?" I ask.

"I think it's really catching on," he says. "I meant to tell you about the young couple who came in recently and had a fit over it when they tasted at the bar."

After I hang up, I laugh out loud. The young couple was John's nephew and his wife who had mentioned to me that they were planning to have dinner at Fleming's for their anniversary. I promised them a bottle of Malbec if they would sidle up to the bar, order a flight of wine, and make a big deal over Tiger Mountain Malbec. Since Jerry has re-ordered from us, at least I know they aren't the only ones who have enjoyed it—even if they were my "plant."

I'll have to tell John about our little marketing coup—if I decide to speak to him ever again.

Just when I finally get another cup of coffee and sit down in my study to write, Coach stops by. The door to our kitchen is always open. I've sometimes thought of putting up sign that reads "Martha is working," but it seems a little snooty for Tiger. I'm sure Coach would disregard it anyhow.

"Maah-tha," he says in his rich Southern accent, "I hope you noticed that I mowed around every clump of orange butterfly weeds in the field so you can pick them for your vases." His grin would destroy even a Scrooge's scowl. The wild butterfly weeds are the brightest of orange hues, and they pop up in the fields at random.

"Thanks, Coach," I reply. "Can we get the far vineyard mowed too? Some wine guys from North Carolina are coming to visit this week. They are starting a big vineyard near Hendersonville."

"I'll try to remember to ask John about it," he says, knowing that "check with John" response is a habit of his that drives me nuts. John will probably nix the mowing this early in the season—a few ragged weeds have never been on his radar, especially since he pays Coach by the hour.

I sit down at the computer again, and Judy drives up. She's just finished the monthly sales report, which looks pretty good since it was such a cold April.

"Wait until you hear this," she says. "We had a call from some addiction rehabilitation center wanting a wine donation for its annual auction and fundraiser. I think we should donate—I may need them; this job could drive me to drink." Her laughter is contagious as always. She leaves me some Greek salad she's made. I put it in the refrigerator for lunch. Judy and I are always trading recipes and dishes, and Greek cooking is her forte.

In fact, Judy's Christmas gift to us last year was one "Judy dinner" a month, delivered to our kitchen. It was the best Christmas gift in the world.

After lunch, I write two paragraphs and hear a knock at the front door. Must be a stranger. Nobody comes to the front door in Tiger.

The visitor is a magazine ad salesman who tells me the gentleman working out there in the vineyard (namely, John) told him to come talk to me. He proceeds to give me the reader profile and all of the grand benefits of advertising with him whether I want to hear such or not. I tell him politely that I have to get some writing done on deadline, and finally he is gone. I eat my lunch salad and hope for some quiet time. More and more I am thinking we need to change John's folksy sign on the tasting room door that tells people if no one is there to "Look for Dr. Ezzard in the vineyards or contact Judy Ruth in the rock house up the hill."

What would I give, when I want to write, for the anonymity of a city Starbucks where I could sit in a corner, sip my favorite vanilla latte, and be left alone.

There's no Starbucks in Tiger, and right now I don't have a laptop. I gave my old one to our son and bought a new PC when I moved to the farm. My thread of thought for writing has now unraveled completely, and I go online to look at laptops and prices. At least I could get out of the house to write; I could go to Grapes and Beans, the coffee shop at Prater's Book Store, or the new Crescent Moon Bakery, all in nearby Clayton and all wireless. But in a small town, people want to chat, and it's impossible not to be interrupted in those favorite hangouts. The Rabun County Library might work—even people I know can't do much talking to me there.

That's exactly what I need to do—buy a laptop and get to the library on some regular schedule. But for the moment, I see Lucy, John's sister, driving up in her red car. She has stopped to give us an extra pan of the lasagna she just made for a church supper.

I answer a dozen e-mails and return a few winery-related phone calls. Then, I make a quick salad and put the lasagna in the oven. At least dinner is taken care of, and John and I don't have to eat it at the same time since I'm still fuming over his cross words this morning. I open a bottle of Norton to go with it, and retreat to my study one more time.

John is watching a baseball game and eating his dinner by the television when I finally decide I will have to tell him about my suggestion to Jerry Sinatra regarding the barrel tasting at the Fleming's wine dinner.

To my utter amazement, he thinks it is a great idea and will help figure out how to make it work.

Then, out of the blue, he says, "I want to be sure we get an invitation for that dinner to my friend John McMullan and his wife. He's really interested in what we're doing and thinks we can put Georgia wine on the map." There is always something special about the way John speaks of his former classmate, but I didn't know then how special John and Marilyn McMullan would become to us.

"I hope you can come out in the Viognier with me tomorrow," he says sheepishly. "I want to show you what I'm doing to revive it from the freeze damage. It's a pretty interesting challenge."

I swirl my customary half glass of dinner wine. "You know, Norton isn't my favorite of our wines, but this is the best Norton you've ever made," I say, sipping on a glass from a new bottle and forgetting that I'm not speaking to him except for sheer business necessity.

"The Norton is selling so well now—I want you to give me two rows to cultivate organically starting this spring," I tell him. "I've already ordered some milky spores to put down for

Japanese beetle eggs, but I want to try not spraying for mildew prevention or even adding any fertilizer on just those two rows.

"Go for it," John says with a grin I haven't seen for a few days. "You know you'll have to hang around here for three years to see if it works—that's how long it takes to even begin to say a vine is 'organically grown.'"

Just when I think this winery is splitting us apart, it glues us back together again, at least temporarily.

22

The Second Bud

Land, then, is not merely soil... —*Aldo Leopold*[15]

I can't sleep. I watch the night show of heavy clouds breaking in silent, jagged lines of light from our bedroom windows, as if signaling new and uneven challenges ahead. I think about the risky decisions John and I have made that brought us to this point, this land, and this wine venture. They are decisions that forever change the trajectory of our lives and our relationship.

Sure enough, our resolve to spend some "down" time together each day is short-lived, as the lasting effects of the devastating freeze become more apparent every day.

John is so intent on "healing" his injured vines that he has no time for my favorite evening vineyard walks. I walk alone across the hayfields at sunset and look back at our turreted roof against sunset puffs of orange and pink. No house in the world could ever be quite as unique. If our grapes are a total loss this season, I don't have an answer to get us out of this dire situation, other than some dramatic move away from the farm.

---

[15] Aldo Leopold, *A Sand County Almanac* (New York: Oxford University Press, 1949) 216.

On my way back to the house, I decide to take the little trail behind the house to the well-worn loop on the mountain above our property. The loop comes down above the new vineyard and the white pines where Poppa planted his Christmas trees for many years. Coach spent a lot of time clearing the narrow trail for me when I first moved to the farm full time. It was his way of saying he was glad I had come home to Tiger—but I know he had misgivings about *Maah-tha* finding more things for him to do every day.

To top off our bad news spring, Coach has been diagnosed with cancer. He called from the ambulance on his way to emergency surgery to make sure his horse, Crown, was going to be fed. He came through the surgery fine, but the doctors found he has a heart problem, too. We worry about him; even though he's in his early eighties, he has always been healthy. I wish I could be as carefree as Coach in appreciating just today. I have a photo of him in the barn with his rooster, his horse and his cat—all he ever needs to feel fulfilled and content.

Weighed down by worry about both Coach's health and the future of our vineyard, I sit on a rock to watch two nuthatches scooting headfirst down the trunk of a hickory tree. They look like wind-up toys run amuck, and I follow their white breasts in and out of the branches as they fly away. I think of the dreadful conversation John and I had last night. He recounted a list of options if we are to sell the farm and winery. First, buy a large loft in Denver—in LoDo, the lower downtown near Larimer Square, which has some new and exciting contemporary architecture. We'd be near our oldest daughter and her family and our Colorado friends. We'd have money and time to travel, especially if one or both of us took up our professional endeavors again on some less strenuous basis. (Of course, that part time or consulting stuff is never really part-time, I reminded John. For a doctor, part-time can still be rewarding; for a lawyer, it equates to paper pushing.) The second alternative he proposed is to do what we've done before, take a really big risk. We could reinvent ourselves again, sell everything, and move to France, either the Bordeaux area or his favorite medieval town of Dinan, in Brittany, only four hours by train from Paris.

"Yeah, but where would we live when we come home—bum in on our grown children?" I asked. That alternative is pie-in-the-sky and he knows it. Since my French is barely good enough to read a menu, and he speaks no French, only a little German, we're not likely to be "employable," even in a wine-related job. What would we live on when our savings ran out?

The last and least appealing option is to figure a way to sell the winery to a third party and enter into a long-term lease agreement to run the vineyards and supply grapes to the winery. But the winery is the entry to our farm and home. What if someone bought it and made it slick and showy instead of the understated farm winery we love? What if they put tacky plastic grapevines around the windows? What if someone paved the grassy parking lot across the road where my sunflowers abound each summer, where round bales of hay dot the fields behind? It would be difficult to drive past it daily—and it would say something to the world about our farm, something that wouldn't be "us."

I couldn't come up with any better alternatives myself other than to go back to some full-time law or writing work in Atlanta, but John doesn't want to live there. He'd rather be in the west near his favorite fly fishing spots—and as cities go, unlike me, he'd take Denver over Atlanta.

Brown. Everything still looks brown from the spring freeze. It's as if we are living a black and white movie, a shattered dream.

Spring in the vineyards is usually a season of anticipation. This year, it's a season of dread. I keep hoping for that annual shot of adrenalin, the infusion of energy that comes with the season's new life. John has pronounced the Tinta Cao, the Portuguese grape that gives our Touriga Nacional wine its flowery nose, "terminal." The Touriga he declares "stunted," and the Viogner, "hopeless."

At the Tiger Post Office, I hear tales of woe all around about orchards and other early crops. It is the first time I can recall even in the years before we took over the farm that our entire blueberry crop is gone. We'll be lucky to have enough berries for one pie.

Even though John and I are both down in the dumps and have taken our despair out on each other with too many harsh words, I finally persuade him to walk with me through the vineyards one evening. It's been two weeks since the awful freeze, but there are some encouraging signs (though they seem precious few). Much of the Malbec, we discover, was not fully budded out and may be okay after all. We are the only Georgia winery making a varietal Malbec, and we sell out of it every year. It's a French-style Malbec, medium-bodied and fruit forward, not the full-bodied, chewy red of the same name that comes out of Argentina (and that is much less expensive). I love some of the Argentine Malbecs, but ours has a certain elegance—and fortunately, our regular wine buyers agree.

We walk past rows of Cabernet Franc, its stately, indented leaves still fragile. It has not really recovered, and even the condition of the Petit Manseng is worrisome. The Tannat may have fared slightly better; it's still hard to tell. It is so prolific that losing some buds may not be all bad. When we start down the rows of Norton, there is no doubt that the late frost didn't harm it at all.

"A native grape is too smart to pop out in early April, despite a warm March," I tell Shelly, who calls, as do all of the children, to console us.

The following week, on a day when John is seeing patients, I decide to join my photographer friend Peter McIntosh and others for a hike up Pinnacle Knob, a special peak near Clayton famously described by naturalist William Bartram in his published travels of 1791. Ever since I read a little of Bartram's eighteenth-century notes and hiked last year on a segment of the Bartram Trail near Highlands, North Carolina, I have been fascinated by his descriptions of the *magnolia fraseri.* Supposedly, he named "Mount Magnolia" what we now know as Pinnacle because of the magnolia species he found there. I rummage through my well-worn Bartram book before I leave to read again the 220-year-old descriptions of the mountain and the deciduous magnolia he found in the thick woods during his visit:

> The exalted peak I named Mount Magnolia, from a new and beautiful species of celebrated family of flowering trees, which here at the cascades of Falling Creek, grows at a high degree of perfection...the leaves spread themselves after a regular order, like the spokes of a wheel, their margins touching or lightly lapping upon each other, form an expansive umbrella superbly crowned with the fragrant flower representing a white plume.[16]

Bartram also mentioned "the pretty grassy vale" with its delightful creek where he took refuge in an Indian cabin near the ancient town of Sticoe, now Clayton, located on Stekoa Creek. The creek's delight has since turned to weeds and pollution, and our winery has agreed to host a fundraiser to assist with efforts to clean it up and create a park along its banks north of town.

The hike is invigorating, and it lifts my sprits to walk through groves of magnolia and rhododendron. Though it's too early for either to be in full bloom, the swelling creamy buds of the magnolia perched atop clusters of giant shiny leaves signal it won't be long. The hike is a leisurely one until the last mile when the trail no longer snakes in gradual ascent. Instead, it is a straight-up path to the peak, a brutal and breathless climb. Along the way, we spot a hooded warbler with yellow breast and head interrupted only by his dark

---

[16] William Bartram, *Travels and Other Writings*, comp. Thomas P. Slaughter (New York: Penguin 1984) 279.

"hood" of a cap. It's a good sign since the hooded warbler, a migrating songbird, returns to the Blue Ridge only when spring is a certainty. I also pick up the familiar sounds of the low-perching ovenbird, a common resident of the farm in spring and summer. I am always listening for what I've been told is its "Southern accent." The ovenbird is known for singing "teacher, teacher," but in the South it supposedly sings "teach, teach."

John is just returning home from a long day of surgery when I arrive at the house. On the kitchen table he leaves a large brown paper bag filled with eleven jars of local honey, mostly my favorite sourwood honey. Then, he changes into his work clothes and is out the door before I can even tell him about my hike. "Check out the honey my patient gave me," he says as he grabs his clippers and green ties for training vines. "Doctors around here would come out better with the old-fashioned bartering system. I'm for it."

He works every night in the vineyards until dark. In the last few days he has stopped talking about our loss of revenue or how much wine we can make. He is focused only on one thing: making his vines healthy again.

Almost every day, when he's not seeing patients, John is up early and out in the vineyards before I can finish my first cup of coffee. One sunny morning in June, I decide to put aside piles of winery paperwork and unanswered e-mails and go help him thin shoots in the Petit Manseng.

"Maybe the freeze damage wasn't as bad as we thought," I say, competing with a mocking bird for John's attention. "William Bartram called him 'the merry mock bird,'" I add, pointing to the branch of a nearby maple tree where the bird sits bullying smaller birds who want to land near the feeder. John just nods and summons me toward the creek to the Malbec vines down the slope from our house. He's encouraged to see that they weren't all budded out when the freeze came and are beginning to look pretty healthy. We pinch off a few tiny hard grapes that are never going to mature, but we stop to admire new clusters on the Mourvedre from second buds formed after the freeze that John is sure will mature.

"Oh, I have some really great news," he says suddenly. "You know I've been talking to some doctors who are potential investors when we buy out the partners. But my good friend John McMullan is willing to negotiate the buyout and invest himself."

I am speechless. There are no more interesting, fun, and generous people in the world than John and Marilyn McMullan. And they know and love fine wine.

Two bluebirds perch on a trellis post and John points to a tiny nest in the recovering green canopy of a Malbec vine. I spot a female purple finch with the zigzag lines on her breast; the male turns bright showy purple, but I decided long ago the female breast pattern has more character.

We end up in the Tannat vines, whose dark green leaves seem truly vibrant and healthy. Big clusters of green berries, though not as many as usual, are forming. I remind John that this is the vineyard where I lost my wedding diamond seven years before.

"That's why you love Tannat," he chuckles.

"And why I talk to it," I respond. He puts his clippers in his pocket and grabs my hand. "And the Petit Manseng told me today it's going to be tangier and sweeter than ever."

Peeking through wispy clouds, a new moon appears over the ridges in the late afternoon sky. As the light begins to fade from the farm's rolling hills, we walk towards our house in the vineyard with a tower, the house that Shelly built to match our crooked mountain. We keep walking silently hand-in-hand—and I'm thinking that like the grapes, our relationship with each other and the farm, has a second bud.

Epilogue

The windows are down and the volume is turned up on my favorite Nora Jones CD as I wheel my pick-up truck down the winding gravel road toward the barn. The crisp September breeze sends ripples across the hayfields, ready for one last fall reaping. Clusters of purple grapes shine with morning dew as I pass the two rows of Norton I'm trying to grow chemical-free.

I sing along with Nora, "When I saw the break of day, I wished that I could fly away...."

Yep—Tiger Mountain is spreading its wings as the winery comes of age—age fourteen to be exact. I drive past the new barn patio where my dream of sipping wine and enjoying an elegant farm-to-table lunch in a refurbished seventy-five-year-old dairy barn became reality this year, thanks in large part to our dear friends, now winery partners, John and Marilyn McMullan. Like us, they are native Georgians who love everything Southern, and they are wine lovers who share our common vision to become the best farm winery ever with our 100 percent locally grown wines.

I bump along the gravel road over the narrow trench John made to keep our gravel from washing away—not exactly scenic, but it works. As I near the production room at the winery, the musky aromas of freshly crushed and fermenting grapes make me want to get my hands into the huge vats of bubbling purple juice again. A banner touting our 2012 gold medal/best of class in the Los Angeles International Wine

Competition waves under the yellow awning in front of the tasting room. It's for John's 2011 Petit Manseng.

I turn onto Old Highway 441 and head toward Tiger. The red-tinged leaves of Poppa's blueberry bushes across the road and the first goldenrod of fall greet my yellow truck with familiar hues.

Things are changing in Tiger, but some things never change. The marquee at the Tiger Drive In announces the last movie of the season, but just across the road, the white clapboard Church of God has been razed to make room for a Tiger city hall although I can't imagine why we need one. The volunteer fire station next door to the drive-in has always been a perfectly fine gathering place. There's another change—a series of connected white frame houses with gabled roofs, porches, and rocking chairs called "Tiger Place"; a new row of shops including one touting kudzu weavings. I turn left at the four-way stop where the Old Store, with Georgia Bulldog birdhouses outside, is sadly advertising a closing sale. Around the corner on the Tiger Connector, I pass the now-deserted Fortune House, a Thai restaurant we welcomed excitedly but which couldn't overcome the native preference for burgers and barbecue. I turn left onto Buzz Saw Lane where I am picking up eight batches of freshly baked cheese straws from Linda's Sweet Treats for a Saturday patio party at the winery. Along the way, I distribute flyers about the next Red Barn wine dinner, featuring the Lake Rabun Hotel's award winning chef, Jamie Allred.

When I return to the vineyards, I spot our daughter Lisa, blond hair blowing in the breeze, helping John unload yellow lugs from the gator along the rows of Viognier we'll start picking in the morning. The bright colored lugs are the plastic tubs we use to haul the harvested grapes to the winery. The vines have rebounded from a light late frost last spring and the clusters of berries, though fewer than usual, are speckled and golden. John and I are reveling in the unexpected joy of having our California teacher-poet daughter return to the farm. What started out as a one-year test to see if she wanted to become a vigneron and vintner like her father has turned into a permanent move. She is to marry an organic farmer, a former attorney who lives nearby. A vineyard wedding is planned; John and I are delighted, as is our whole family.

I stop to snip a few of the season's last buds from my rose bushes on the road from the barn, making a mental note to get a frame for the pictures of Coach and his horse, Crown, that I want to hang in the barn entry. He died several years ago, but his spirit lives on in the red barn he loved so much. It seems only yesterday that we planted the first rose bushes with Coach's help. Another "leaf," as the years are termed in the life of grape vines, is coming round—and so is another wondrous harvest. I leave my truck by the barn and walk up the winding gravel road to the house Shelly built in the vineyard—that's how we describe our home that she designed. I pass the grandchildren's arboretum, its trees carefully labeled with little metal signs for each of the six grandchildren—and the seventh, a newly planted dogwood, for John Jr.'s beloved black Lab. It was planted at the request of our youngest grandchild, Trimble James ("T.J.," named for his two great-grandfathers), who can't remember life without his dog. The grandchildren's arboretum symbolizes the seventh generation on our farm, but for now, we're happy that our three children, the sixth generation, seem to be as in love with the land as we are.

John stops by in the gator to see if I want to help him measure Tannat sugars. "Not until I put my new ring away at the house," I say playfully. (In an emotional moment, John recently gave me a new diamond ring to replace the wedding diamond lost somewhere in the Tannat vines the year we first planted.) We pass the Malbec vines, leaves already beginning to drop as if to say their work is done. Always the first to ripen, they're the only grapes we have harvested so far.

"Hurry," says John, as I head to the house on foot. "I can't wait to see if the Tannat are as perfect as I think they may be." It's as if he'd never picked them before. But harvest is like that, our vines sharing their peak energy with us.

We have come full circle to another harvest, each unlike any of the previous. The seasons of our lives are the seasons of the grape. May it always be so.

Index